Burundi: The Hutu and The Tutsi Cauldron of Conflict and Quest for Dynamic Compromise

Godfrey Mwakikagile

1

Burundi: The Hutu and The Tutsi
Cauldron of Conflict and Quest for Dynamic Compromise

First Edition

ISBN 978-9987-16-031-0

New Africa Press
Dar es Salaam, Tanzania

Contents

Special note

I WROTE this book more than ten years ago. It was accepted for publication during that time by my publisher who had already published five of my books between 1999 and 2001.

Although I signed a contract with the publisher, I decided to cancel it for a number of reasons and have my work published elsewhere.

But instead of pursuing the project, I set it aside until now, as I continued to write other books.

The work is essentially the same as it was more than ten years ago when I first wrote it. And I wanted to keep it that way to retain and reflect the times and context in which I wrote it, including the sources I cited during that period to document this study. In that sense, it is a work from the past. But it is also for the present.

There is very little change in terms of content and the work's central thesis, except for a few things – in fact very few – which I have added here and there in different parts of the book. And you can tell what they are based on the dated material I have cited for further documentation of my work which is "frozen" in time.

Acknowledgements

THE EXECUTION of this project owes its completion to many individuals and institutions especially in Africa, Britain and the United States.

They include journalists and academics, African leaders and ordinary citizens, civic and religious organisations as well as human rights groups and the United Nations, all of whom have been an indispensable source of information I have used in different contexts to document my work.

I wish to express my profound gratitude to them all. And I take full responsible for any mistakes in terms of analysis and factual presentation which may be found in my work.

Introduction

THIS WORK looks at conflicts between the Hutu and the Tutsi in Burundi.

It is an abridged version of my forthcoming book, *Civil Wars in Rwanda and Burundi: Conflict Resolution in Africa.*

The bloodiest conflicts between the Hutu and Tutsi started in the early sixties soon after the country won independence from Belgium. They continued through the nineties and beyond.

My work is placed in a broader regional context of which Burundi is an integral part. The countries in the region are Rwanda, the Democratic Republic of Congo, Uganda and Tanzania which have also been embroiled in the conflict in varying degrees because of the rivalries between the Hutu and the Tutsi in Rwanda, Burundi and eastern Congo.

It also provides a comprehensive look, in telescopic form, at the rebellions in eastern Congo in which Rwanda, Uganda and Burundi were deeply involved and which eventually led to the ouster of President Mobutu Sese Seseko, one of the longest-ruling leaders in post-colonial Africa.

The fall of Mobutu heralded the dawn of a new era for the entire region. But it also contributed to a wider regional conflict which came to be known as "Africa's world war."

The conflict between the Hutu and the Tutsi in both Rwanda and Burundi played a critical role in igniting this regional war.

My work also looks at attempts by Burundi's neighbours to resolve the conflict in that country whose driving force was Julius Nyerere, the former president of Tanzania. Unfortunately, he died before peace was achieved in Burundi.

The conflict between the Hutu and the Tutsi is one of Africa's intractable problems. It is also one of the oldest in the post-colonial era.

Its resolution will largely depend on dynamic comprise, the kind of concessions which have never been made before by both sides. It will also require innovative solutions and will be a major achievement in conflict resolution in Africa.

Part One:

The Killing Fields of Africa:
Background and Aftermath

THE 1994 RWANDAN GENOCIDE in which about one million Tutsis and their Hutu sympathisers were massacred triggered a chain of events which plunged the entire Great Lakes region of East-Central Africa into turmoil on a scale never witnessed before.

This chapter attempts to comprehend the complex web of events and interrelated forces that led to the upheaval and shaped the context in which the future of the region will be determined for many years, as the countries involved remain trapped in a vicious cycle of violence and a chronic state of instability.

Just before the remaining Tutsis in Rwanda were to be wiped out, their brethren in the Rwandan Patriotic Front

(RPF) – an army of Tutsi exiles and some Hutus – invaded the country from their bases in Uganda and seized power from the genocidal Hutu regime which instigated the massacres. The remaining Tutsis were saved. But the violence continued.

The collapse of the Hutu ethnocracy whose army was routed by the RPF triggered a massive exodus of Hutus who feared reprisals at the hands of the new Tutsi rulers. About 2 million Hutus fled to neighbouring Zaire (renamed the Democratic Republic of Congo) and Tanzania.

Most of them sought refuge in Zaire which soon became the scene of more massacres of genocidal proportions; this time, directed against the Hutu refugees who perished at the hands of their Tutsi conquerors exacting retribution for the atrocities perpetrated against their kinsmen in the Rwandan genocide. They went in hot pursuit of the Hutus.

Thus, what started out as a genocidal campaign by the Rwandan Hutu regime and its extremist supporters to exterminate the Tutsi also led to a genocidal rampage against hundreds of thousands of innocent Hutu civilians including the perpetrators of the 1994 genocide and plunged the entire region into chaos.

Regional Imbroglio

The root cause of all this violence and regional instability is exclusion from power of one group by the other, mostly the Hutu by the Tutsi.

Hutus constitute the vast majority of the population (at least 85%) in both Rwanda and Burundi where the two groups have been in conflict at different times during the past 400 years even when some of the conflicts have not escalated into violence or full-scale war.

Yet, in spite of their minority status, it is the Tutsi who

have held power in both countries except for 32 years in Rwanda where the Hutu ruled from 1962 – when the country won independence from Belgium – until 1994 when they were ousted by the invading force of the Tutsi-dominated Rwandan Patriotic Front (RPF). And the regional dimension of the conflict can be directly attributed to the security threat posed by the Hutu rebels to the Tutsi-dominated states of Rwanda and Burundi, and by Ugandan insurgents trying to overthrow the government of their country.

The conflict also assumed regional proportions because of the expansionist ambitions of both Rwanda and Uganda, and to a smaller extent Burundi, to annex parts of eastern Congo ostensibly to create a buffer zone and secure their borders. But the creation of such a "security corridor," if successful, would only perpetuate conflict and take the war deeper into Congo.

The conflict in the Great Lakes region assumed a much wider dimension when neighbouring countries – Rwanda, Uganda and Burundi – supported a rebellion launched by a coalition of forces to oust Zaire's long-ruling dictator Mobutu Sese Seko from power.

The insurgency was spearheaded by Tutsi-led forces whose nominal head was Laurent Kabila, a member of the Luba ethnic group from the northern part of Shaba Province which was renamed Katanga.

The rebel army was organised by Rwandan leaders. They are also the ones who chose Kabila to be the leader of the rebel movement, hoping that he would be more friendly to them than Mobutu was, once he became president of Zaire.

Kabila seized power in May 1997 and renamed the country the Democratic Republic of Congo (DRC).

During his first months in office, Kabila worked closely with Rwandan and Ugandan leaders, mostly out of sheer necessity. He owed his rise to power to the leaders of those two countries. And he remained in power because of the protection provided to him by Rwandan Tutsi soldiers who masterminded the military campaign that ousted Mobutu and remained in Kinshasa, Congo's capital, to help him consolidate his rule.

But Kabila did not become the kind of leader Rwanda and Uganda thought they would have. They thought they would be able to control and manipulate him. Like any true nationalist, he resented outside control. And there was strong resentment across Congo against Rwandan Tutsis whose presence in the capital Kinshasa was interpreted by many Congolese as a violation of their sovereignty, with Rwandans being seen as an occupation army on conquered territory. It was the ultimate insult.

Both Rwanda and Uganda, as well as Burundi which was ruled by the Tutsi like Rwanda, also became disillusioned with Kabila even in the early months of his rule because he failed or simply refused to restrain – it was actually a combination of both – the Hutu rebels and Ugandan insurgents based in eastern Congo from attacking them.

It was this security threat which prompted Rwanda and Uganda, with the assistance of Burundi, to organise a rebellion and directly intervene in Congo in an attempt to overthrow Kabila and replace him with a more friendly Congolese government which would take the security interests of the three countries into account.

The rebellion started in August 1998 when President Kabila expelled Rwandan Tutsi soldiers from Kinshasa. Rwanda, Uganda, and Burundi intervened immediately, although they denied such involvement until later when they admitted that.

Kabila got a lot of help from his allies to resist the invasion. Angola, Zimbabwe, Namibia, Chad, and Sudan sent troops and weapons to bolster Congo's fragile army and got directly involved in combat against the rebels who were supported by Rwanda and Uganda. Burundi also supported the insurgents although it was Rwanda which played the biggest role.

None of that would have happened had the Tutsi in Rwanda and Burundi agreed to share power – on meaningful basis – with the Hutu majority in those two countries.

There would have been no Hutu rebels operating from Congo in an attempt to dislodge the Tutsi minority from power, and therefore no need for Rwanda and Burundi to try and neutralise them by invading Congo where the rebels were based; an invasion which drew in other national armies in what came to be Africa's most internationalised conflict which had its origin in the 1994 Rwandan genocide and the Hutu-Tutsi conflict in Burundi. The conflict came to be known as "Africa's World War."

The Rwandan genocide itself – instigated by Hutu leaders and the academic elite who, considering their history of hundreds of years of Hutu domination by the Tutsi, did not want and were afraid to share power with their "historical enemies" – can be traced back to the mass uprising by the Hutu against their Tutsi aristocratic rulers in November 1959; and to the repeated attempts by the Tutsi during most of the next 35 years to regain the power they lost in that peasant uprising which could even be called a peasant revolution since it led to fundamental change in terms of who later ruled Rwanda after the Tutsi were ousted. The Hutu finally seized power.

Compounding the problem is the centuries-old hatred or mistrust between the two groups – whether some people want to admit it or not – which, like the desire to monopolise power on an ethnic basis, contributed to the genocide. As many Hutu leaders publicly stated just before and during the 1994 massacres of the Tutsi, the biggest mistake that the Hutu made during the 1959 mass uprising was that they did not wipe out the Tutsi; a job they urged their followers to finish in 1994.

During the 1959 Hutu uprising, more than 100,000 Tutsis were massacred in what was indeed a genocide but

17

whose magnitude was overshadowed 35 years later by the 1994 holocaust.

Many Hutus, probably the majority, never regretted the massacre of the Tutsi. As Professor Leon Mugesira, a renowned Hutu historian at the Rwandan National University in Butare, told a Hutu extremist gathering in November 1992 almost exactly 33 years after the 1959 mass uprising by the Hutu against the Tutsi:

"The fatal mistake we made in 1959 was to let the Tutsi get out....We have to act. Wipe them all out!"[1]

Calls for Tutsi extermination were also made in newspapers, on the radio and on television – but mostly by word of mouth – to incite Hutus across the country to isolate and kill their Tutsi neighbours, friends and any other Tutsis including their own relatives and children who were half-Tutsi or who had any identifiable Tutsi lineage. For example, *Kangura*, a Hutu newspaper edited by Hassan Ngeze, listed the "Hutu ten commandments" which included isolating the "evil" Tutsis and condemned intermarriage with them as a pollution of "pure Hutu."[2] And the Hutu-edited *La Medaille*, a magazine, stated in its February 1994 edition, not long before the massacres started in April, that "the Tutsi race could be extinguished."[3]

But the most virulent and effective campaign was carried out by Radio/Television Libre des Mille Collines (RTLM) because of its wide coverage across the country and its ability to transmit its message of hate and incitement to every Hutu including illiterates who could not read the newspapers. And educated Hutus played a critical role in this campaign of genocide. As Kenyan Professor Michael Chege stated:

"The radio's intellectual braintrust was made up of Ferdinand Nahimana, a professor of history at the

Rwandan National University at Butare, and Casimir Bizimungu, the articulate multilingual foreign minister of a former government, and the manager of this 'independent' radio station.

Indeed, so strong was the academic input...that, after the massacres, Emmanuel Bugingo, the new and irreproachable rector of the Butare campus, confessed that 'all the killing in Rwanda was carefully planned by intellectuals and those intellectuals passed through this university.'"[4]

Coincidentally, but in a chilling way, the nearly one million Tutsis who were exterminated in 1994 were "replaced" by one million Tutsis who returned from exile in Uganda.

Other returnees came from Burundi and Tanzania. But most of them came from Uganda. They included many who were born in exile, returning with their parents who fled Rwanda in 1959 as adults or as children. One of the exiles was Paul Kagame, Rwanda's vice president and defence minister and the country's *de facto* ruler, who fled to Uganda with his parents when he was two years old.

The Rwandan Patriotic Front (RPF) ousted the murderous Hutu regime in July 1994, only to institute another tyranny; this time, an ethnocracy dominated by the Tutsi who went on to launch their own campaign of terror against the Hutu majority.

It was systematic, yet indiscriminate, in its retaliation against the Hutu for the extermination of one million Tutsis and their Hutu sympathisers.

Countless innocent Hutu civilians were murdered during the following years. They included innocent women, children and the elderly, ostensibly in a search-and-destroy mission directed against the perpetrators of the 1994 genocide.

The retaliatory campaign continues today, cold and calculated, pursued with malicious vindictiveness. The result of this government-sponsored terror and exclusion of the Hutu majority from power is increased polarisation between the two ethnic groups that are already divided by intense hatred and deep mistrust in Africa's most densely populated country; with the two "historical enemies" living side by side as they have for the past 400 years in a feudal relationship dominated by the Tutsi.

Exclusion of the Hutu majority from power, again by the Tutsi, also explains Burundi's descent into chaos including the 1972 genocide against the Hutu.

Burundi, Africa's second most populous country, is almost an exact mirror image of Rwanda – its neighbouring twin state to the north – both in terms of ethnic composition and troubled history.

Oppression of the Hutu by the Tutsi in Burundi led to a Hutu uprising in 1972 – 1973 which claimed 10,000 Tutsi lives. The Tutsi retaliated and massacred more than 200,000 Hutus within three months.

In an attempt to eliminate the Hutu threat to their hegemonic control of the country, they also killed every Hutu who had secondary school education, a government job, and money. Most of them were killed in 1972, the year of the biggest uprising.

Yet hardly anyone talks about this genocide by the Tutsi against the Hutu in Burundi which took place 22 years before Rwanda's 1994 genocide, and was just one among several massacres of genocidal proportions perpetrated by the Tutsi against the Hutu through the years including the massacre of more than 200,000 Rwandan Hutu refugees in the late 1990s in Zaire whose fate was inextricably linked to what had been going on in both Rwanda and Burundi. As Professor René Lemarchand states in "The Fire in the Great Lakes":

"Today the 1972 Burundi genocide has fallen into virtual oblivion – except among the Hutu masses – yet its significance is crucial to understanding subsequent events in both Burundi and Rwanda.

Although the magnitude of the Rwanda holocaust is without precedent – it is estimated to have caused the deaths of a million people – the killing of tens of thousands of Hutu refugees at the hands of the Rwandan Patriotic Army (RPA, the armed forces of the RPF government) in eastern Congo in 1996 and 1997 can be considered a third holocaust (after Burundi's 1972 and Rwanda's 1994 genocides)....

As many as 200,000 Hutu refugees may have been killed by RPA troops and Kabila's rebel army...(and) as many as 300,000 must have died of starvation and disease...in Zaire....And to this might be added the Kibeho killings, perpetrated inside Rwanda in April 1995, when at least 5,000 Hutu refugees were killed in cold blood by RPA units."[5]

A discussion of Hutu massacres by the Tutsi is not in any way intended to justify or provide an excuse of the extermination of nearly one million Tutsis in Rwanda in 1994. It is, rather, an attempt to understand why that genocide took place by putting it in the broader context of the volatile ethnic politics of the region (in both Rwanda and Burundi whose fates are inextricably linked) and the long history of antagonism between the two groups.

Traditionally, the Hutu and the Tutsi in both countries have had a lord-serf relationship for centuries, with the Hutu tending the farmlands and cattle owned by the Tutsi. The imposition of this overlordship on the Hutu by the Tutsi still rankles the vast majority of the Hutu who have been relegated to an inferior status in their own homeland and have worked for the Tutsi as virtual slaves for 400 years.

Any attempt to ignore or gloss over this unsavoury part of history makes it impossible for anybody to comprehend the enmity and deep mistrust between the two groups which has surfaced in recent years; and why the Hutu revolted against their Tutsi aristocratic rulers in Rwanda in November 1959; also why the Tutsi in Burundi have slaughtered hundreds of thousands – probably one million Hutus since 1972 alone; and why the 1994 Rwandan genocide – in which nearly one million Tutsis were exterminated – took place.

A look at the massacre of the Hutu by the Tutsi in both Rwanda and Burundi, and in what was then Zaire, through the years is also intended to show that the 1994 Rwandan genocide, tragic as it was, did not occur in a vacuum and is not the only large-scale massacre which has taken place in this highly combustible region. It is also intended to show the combustible elements, and the context, which led to that explosion.

It is true that the near-extermination of the entire Tutsi population in the Rwandan genocide is unprecedented in its magnitude although not in its motives. But simply because it is unprecedented in terms of magnitude does not mean that we should lose proportional perspective on reality, out of lopsided sympathy for the victims of that holocaust, while ignoring or overlooking the suffering of others, the Hutu, and the atrocities committed against them by the Tutsi in both Rwanda and Burundi through the years, and why they are fighting.

To ascribe ulterior motives – or of a bestial nature – to their struggle for inclusion in the political process, however excessive some of the means they have employed in pursuit of their goal, does not portray them or their enemies fairly; nor does it facilitate the quest for peace and stability in the region. For example, Philip Gourevitch who is the author of *We Wish to Inform You That Tomorrow We Will Be Killed With Our Families* which is otherwise a well-balanced account, stated in his article, "The Psychology of Slaughter," in *The New York Times*:

"The killers...are usually described as 'Hutu rebels,' a label that suggests they are fighting for something. In fact, these terrorists have no identifiable cause, no idea other than rape, pillage and mass murder....

The prospect of overcoming the Hutu terrorist scourge remains remote. According to United Nations estimates, as many as 30,000 of these terrorists remain active in Central Africa.

The vast majority of them...are based in Congo, under the patronage of President Laurent Kabila...(who) has made these forces into a cornerstone of his defense forces.

Yet there is no great international outcry against him, or his many allies – including South Africa – for being in league with the most horrific political criminals on the continent....

And as Rwanda prepares to commemorate the fifth anniversary of the start of the genocide, on April 6, one can't help wondering whether the end is in sight."[6]

It is interesting to note that although Gourevitch contends that these Hutu fighters have no identifiable cause which they are fighting for, and are no more than outright rapists, pillagers and mass murderers, he contradicts himself – obviously inadvertently – when he goes on to describe them as "political criminals," thus implicitly admitting that their crimes are politically motivated. Nelson Mandela was imprisoned for almost 30 years as a political prisoner. He and his compatriots were a even described by the apartheid regime and its supporters as a terrorists. Yet they had an identifiable and just cause they were fighting for.

If the crimes of the Hutu rebels are indeed politically motivated, as most of them are, in order to bring about fundamental political change contrary to what Gourevitch says, then the label "rebels" is appropriate in this context as a way of describing them since they have rebelled against authority and are fighting for something: to overthrow the Tutsi-dominated governments which are oppressing Hutus in both Rwanda and Burundi.

It is, of course true, as Gourevitch contends, that we can't help wondering whether or not the end to these massacres is in sight; not only in Rwanda but also in Burundi; and not only of the Tutsi by the Hutu but also of the Hutu by the Tutsi – probably even more so.

The brutal excesses committed by the Hutu rebels – and by the Tutsi-dominated armies and security forces against Hutu civilians in both Rwanda and Burundi – can not be excused or condoned; although, depending on the context, one man's terrorist is another man's freedom fighter: from Menachem Begin and Moshe Dayan in Israel to Nelson Mandela, Oliver Tambo, Robert Mangaliso Sobukwe, Walter Sisulu and Govan Mbeki in South Africa; from Dedan Kimathi in Kenya to Josiah Tongogara, Edgar Tekere, Robert Mugabe and Joshua Nkomo in Zimbabwe; from Amilcar Cabral in Guinea-Bissau to Samora Machel in Mozambique. The list goes on and on.

The fundamental question that should be addressed is: Why are tens of thousands of Hutus fighting in both Rwanda and Burundi? Just to rape, loot and kill as Gourevitch and others contend?

Is that why they risk their lives and those of their families?

Is that why they seek international support for their struggle and understanding of their cause?

And is that the reason why hundreds of thousands of Hutus, most of them civilians, have fled their home countries and sought refuge in Congo and Tanzania through the years?

Is there no other motive behind the Hutu rebel attacks? Is the armed struggle by the rebels not being waged in pursuit of political objectives?

Wasn't the assassination of the first democratically elected president of Burundi, Melchior Ndadaye, a Hutu, in October 1993 by Tutsi soldiers who bayoneted him to death, enough reason to provoke many Hutus even some of the most timid ones – "enough is enough" – into violence in retaliation for the murder, given their history of oppression by the Tutsi?

Would the 1994 Rwandan genocide have taken place had the Hutu not been oppressed and exploited, virtually enslaved, by the Tutsi for 400 years in both Rwanda and Burundi?

Would it have occurred if the Tutsi-dominated Rwandan Patriotic Front (RPF) did not invade Rwanda from Uganda for the first time in October 1990, posing a threat to the Hutu?

In the late 1990s, President Benjamin Mkapa of Tanzania once described the attacks by the Hutus rebels as "military expressions of political intent." By saying so, he was not trying to justify the attacks but was trying to explain what motivated the rebels in many – if not in most – cases to launch such attacks against the dominant group, the Tutsi, who were the rulers of both countries.

There probably were some Hutu rebels who had no political agenda and were motivated purely by ethnic hatred in attacking Tutsis, although even such attacks can not in all cases be attributed to sheer hatred of the Tutsi without any political motivation.

To dismiss all Hutu rebels as nothing but a bunch of killers without any political agenda or aspirations is being utterly simplistic.

In many cases, Rwanda is Burundi, and Burundi is Rwanda. It is a tangled web. What happens in one country very often affects the other. The conflicts feed on each other. As Lemarchand states:

"The 1972 genocide (in Burundi) had 'cleansed' the country of all educated Hutu elites – including secondary school and university students – allowing the rise of a solidly entrenched Tutsi ethnocracy.

It is thus easy to see why the assassination of Burundi's Hutu President Ndadaye in 1993 was viewed by many

Tutsi hard-liners as the quickest way to ward off the threat posed to their hegemony; what was not anticipated was the outburst of rage that seized the Hutu population in the face of an event that conjured up memories of 1972.

After killing thousands of Tutsi civilians in October 1993, some 300,000 Hutus fled to Rwanda to escape an extremely brutal repression by the (Tutsi) army. It is reasonable to assume that a great many joined hands with the Interahamwe during the 1994 (Rwandan) genocide, before seeking refuge in Congo or Tanzania, or returning to Burundi."[7]

Many of these tragedies through the years in both Rwanda and Burundi could have been avoided – or at the very least they could have been mitigated – if the ruling Tutsis had agreed to genuine power sharing with the Hutu majority on the basis of proportional representation; taking into account legitimate fears and concerns of the Tutsi minority that they would be exterminated (in retaliation for their oppression and exploitation of the Hutu for centuries, although that is something the Tutsi would not admit but would instead contend that the Hutu would exterminate them simply because they hated them); and accommodating the interests and genuine aspirations of the Hutu majority who have been denied the right to participate in the political process on democratic basis.

And the 1994 Rwandan genocide could have been avoided if the Hutu – who were in power for 32 years from July 1962 to July 1994 – had agreed back in the 1960s, soon after independence, to share power with the Tutsi on meaningful basis instead of excluding them and consigning them to subordinate status.

Democracy on the basis of majority rule is totally out of the question in that context. It will exclude the Tutsi minority from power – they will never win a democratic election against the Hutu majority – and will guarantee hegemonic control of both Rwanda and Burundi by the

Hutu forever.

That is what the Hutu attempted to do in Rwanda in the mass uprising of November 1959 (assume full control of the country), with tragic consequences for the entire region during the following decades, which culminated in the 1994 genocide of the Tutsi.

The Rwandan holocaust in turn led to a wider conflict that engulfed the entire Great Lakes region and the heart of Africa, Congo, involving national armies from nine African countries: Congo itself, Rwanda, Uganda, Burundi, Angola, Zimbabwe, Namibia, Chad, and Sudan, and at least 20 rebel and militia groups including the Angola rebels of UNITA, a Portuguese acronym for National Union for the Total Independence of Angola.

But even before the multinational conflict erupted in 1998, with Congo as the battleground, the Great Lakes region had already been the scene of massive bloodshed between the Hutu and the Tutsi since 1962 when both Rwanda and Burundi won independence from Belgium. While the Tutsi in Burundi thwarted attempts by the Hutu majority to become the rulers of the newly independent nation on democratic basis – given their numerical preponderance, victory for the Hutu was a foregone conclusion – and therefore remained in control; their kinsmen in Rwanda had been sidelined since the 1959 Hutu mass uprising and never even had the initiative to position themselves in an advantageous position to assume power at independence.

Therefore, when independence came, the Hutu automatically became the new rulers of Rwanda, with tens of thousands of Tutsis and their aristocratic elite having fled into exile. And every major political event in the region during the next three decades was, in one way or another, linked to the 1959 Hutu uprising:

"Each event of political significance in the region during those 32 years (1962 – 1994) was related to the

27

(1959) Rwandan revolution: the fall of two monarchies – Rwanda in 1962, Burundi in 1966; the assassination of two leading Hutu personalities in Burundi – Prime Minister Pierre Ngendadumwe in 1965, and President Melchior Ndadaye in 1993; several military takeovers – the 1973 coup in Rwanda and the 1965, 1976, 1987, and 1996 coups in Burundi; the 1972 Burundi genocide of Hutus; the rural uprising in North Kivu (Zaire) in 1993; the 1990 invasion of Rwanda by RPF (the Tutsi Rwandan Patriotic Front from its bases in Uganda), and the 1994 genocide of Tutsis and moderate Hutus; and the transformation of North and South Kivu (provinces in eastern Zaire) into a privileged sanctuary for Hutu-sponsored border raids into Rwanda – and ultimately, into a killing ground for fleeing Hutu refugees (by Rwandan Tutsi soldiers and Zairean Tutsi rebels allied with their Rwandan kinsmen)."[8]

Another Hutu prime minister of Burundi, Joseph Bamina who succeeded Ngendadumwe, was assassinated later in 1965 after an uprising by the Hutu against Tutsi domination failed. Bamina was a member of the Tutsi political party, UPRONA (*Union pour le Progrès national* – the Union for National Progress) which dominated the country.

The success of the 1959 mass uprising by the Hutu in Rwanda raised hope among the Hutu in both Rwanda and Burundi that they had the capacity to free themselves from their Tutsi oppressors, and that they would one day become the rulers of the two countries as they indeed succeeded in doing in Rwanda from 1962 to 1994.

The 1959 peasant revolution also inspired a significant number of Hutus to take bold initiatives to achieve their goals and radicalised many of them into a potent political force ready to take up arms to end Tutsi supremacy.

But it also frightened the Tutsi minority who feared that they were about to be dominated and possibly exterminated by the Hutu majority whom they knew they had been oppressing for centuries, unless they did something to stave off the Hutu onslaught.

To ward off this danger, the Tutsi resorted to brutal repression and large-scale massacres of the Hutu in Burundi where the Tutsi were still in control. The country won independence on 1 July 1962 under an absolute Tutsi monarchy and changed its name from Urundi to Burundi.

The situation was different in Rwanda. There, the rise of the Hutu to power at independence, also on 1 July 1962 – the country was until then called Ruanda, not Rwanda – triggered another exodus of the Tutsi, following the first one in 1959 when the Hutu emerged victorious in a mass uprising which toppled the Tutsi aristocracy.

But there were also similarities. In Burundi, consolidation of power and increased repression by the Tutsi aristocratic rulers and the Tutsi army in the early 1960s led to an exodus – reminiscent of the 1959 Tutsi exodus from Rwanda – of tens of thousands of Hutus to Rwanda which was then under Hutu leadership, and to Tanganyika which was renamed Tanzania on 29 October 1964 after uniting with Zanzibar on 26 April in the same year.

Many Hutu politicians in Burundi dreamt of transforming that aristocratic state into a republican one like neighbouring Rwanda where their kinsmen were firmly entrenched and exercised virtual absolute power over the Tutsi.

But prospects for such fundamental change remained bleak. The Tutsi were in full control in Burundi. And their fear of Hutu majority rule was heightened when their brethren, tens of thousands of them (at least 100,000), fled Rwanda and sought refuge in Burundi in the wake of the 1959 mass uprising which effectively ended about 400 years of Tutsi aristocratic rule and replaced it with a Hutu-dominated republican form of government at independence in 1962. Their fear was also compounded by the exclusion of their kinsmen from power in Rwanda where the Hutu assumed full control of the country soon after the Belgian colonial rulers left.

The fleeing Tutsis recounted horror stories of what happened to them in Rwanda at the hands of the Hutu in the 1959 revolution, inflaming passions among their kinsmen in Burundi. Burundi's Tutsis vowed they would never allow that to happen to them and welcomed their brethren with open arms.

In due course, Burundi was to become a launching pad for military raids into Rwanda by these Tutsi exiles who were determined to overthrow the Hutu and regain power in their homeland which they lost in 1959. Naturally, the incursions provoked a retaliatory response by the Hutu against the Tutsi who remained in Rwanda, forcing more to flee to Burundi, Uganda, Congo, and Tanzania.

But it was a flight – into forced exile – which also had combustible elements. For example, the 20,000 Tutsi refugees from Rwanda who settled in eastern Congo in the early 1960s inflamed passions among the members of the local tribes who were hostile to immigrants from Rwanda – Tutsis as well as Hutus (there even some from Burundi) – who had lived in the region since precolonial times.

Rwandan Tutsis first settled in the area – what came to be known as eastern Congo – in the 1700s. And the 1959 revolution in Rwanda only made things worse for them by forcing them into exile in some places where they were not welcome, especially eastern Congo and Uganda.

Hostility towards them only intensified through the decades. In 1982, Rwanda appealed for international help when Uganda uprooted about 25,000 Rwandan – mostly Tutsi – immigrants, burning their homes and stealing their cattle. Thousands fled back to Rwanda, pleading for help – food and shelter.[9] And through the years, the Tutsi government of Burundi also accused the Hutu government of Rwanda of massacring Tutsis.

In turn, the Rwandan government accused Burundi of

harbouring Tutsi guerrillas who were trying to overthrow it and re-institute a Tutsi ethnocracy in Rwanda.

Both were credible charges.

Besides attempting to overthrow the Hutu government in Rwanda from their bases in Burundi, the Tutsi refugees from the 1959 Rwandan Hutu mass uprising also got involved in another major political struggle and military activity. These were the refugees who settled in eastern Congo, and their involvement had to do with a rebellion going on in that country against the central government.

But unlike their kinsmen who settled in Burundi where fellow Tutsis were in control of the country, the Rwandan Tutsis who had sought refuge in eastern Congo found no indigenous ethnic constituency comparable in stature and power to the Tutsi ethnic base in Burundi which could provide them with shelter and help them pursue their objectives, in spite of the fact that many Tutsis – mostly from Rwanda – had been living in Congo since the 1700s.

Although they had lived there for a long time, they still were in a precarious position. They were not powerful. And the local tribes had always been hostile towards them, although they themselves were, historically speaking, native to the region, having lived there for about 200years after they migrated from Rwanda. As Vincent Gasana and Alfred Ndahiro stated in their report, "Zaire Crisis Provokes Tribalism," in *Africa Analysis*:

"Long before the conflict in eastern Zaire developed into a full-blown war, the little-known Banyamurenge (also known as Banyamulenge) had been trying to make their point: they want to go on living quietly as they have done for centuries, away not from the rest of the world, but from the rest of the Zaireans....

Their story starts in the 16th century, when King Kigeri Nyamuheshera of Rwanda sent a group of Rwandan families to occupy the newly-conquered area of Bunyabungo, present-day Uvira.

There was a second wave and a third followed in the 19th century.

As Batutsi, the Banyamurenge were pastoralists. They moved and settled in the high altitude area of eastern Zaire to protect their cattle from disease and themselves from local Zairean hostility. They evolved a highly organised, inter-linked community. To this very day, their adherence to traditional forms of communication, means that no sooner does a stranger arrive in their area than his presence is communicated throughout the while community.

The modern state of Zaire never acknowledged them as Zaireans. They asked and got nothing from the Zairean government....

There have been periodic attempts by their Zairean neighbours to dislodge them from their lands. These were always repulsed by force of arms. Their martial prowess and skilful use of bows and arrows has long been passed into the region's folkrole.

Every Zairean, Rwandan and Murundi child will tell you how the Banyamurenge can shoot a fly off you with an arrow and leave you unscathed.

Such fairy tales bolstered by frequent victories against their attackers enabled the Banyamurenge to live unmolested until recently.

Following the first ethnic massacres in Rwanda in 1959, large numbers of Batutsi fled to neighbouring countries, including Zaire (then known as Congo). Though sympathetic, the Banyamurenge wanted to keep their distinct identity. But the Zaireans lumped them together and refused to recognise any distinction. The 1990 – 94 Rwandan civil war further complicated the situation."[10]

Although the Tutsi refugees who settled in eastern Congo after they fled Rwanda in the wake of the 1959 Hutu uprising found no large ethnic constituency of fellow Tutsis who could provide them with sanctuary in Congo and forge links with them in pursuit of a common cause, they did find a different ally: the followers of the late Congolese prime minister, Patrice Lumumba, who were fighting a guerrilla war in an attempt to oust the central government installed by the CIA which masterminded Lumumba's assassination.

The rebellion in eastern Congo was known as a Mulelist insurgency which started in 1964. It was named after Pierre Mulele, Lumumba's 35-year-old education minister and heir-apparent, although he did not lead this particular insurrection in the east. He led an insurgency in Kwilu Province in western Congo from 1963 – 1968, while the eastern insurrection was led by Gaston Soumialot who was assisted by Nicolas Olenga and Laurent Kabila.[11]

The Tutsi refugees from the 1959 Rwandan uprising allied themselves with the pro-Lumumbist rebels in eastern Congo out of necessity in order to secure the support which they hoped they would get one day and enable them to regain power in their homeland. But it was a matter of expediency on both sides.

Many of those rebels in the eastern part of Congo were Tutsi. They were led by Joseph Mudandi who was trained in guerrilla warfare in China together with several other Rwandan Tutsis who had fled their homeland.

China had also intervened in Burundi's ethnic conflict by supporting the Tutsi. In 1963, the Chinese trained a number of Tutsis in guerrilla warfare in China. The massacres that followed, mostly of the Hutu by the Tutsi in Burundi, were thus facilitated by China, earning the Chinese a bad reputation in African circles beyond Burundi.

The Chinese committed the same blunder in Rwanda when in the same year, 1963, they supported Tutsi guerrillas who invaded their homeland in an attempt to overthrow the Hutu-dominated government. The Tutsi guerrillas killed more than 20,000 Hutus, mostly civilians, in that invasion which they launched from their bases in Burundi.

In eastern Congo, hundreds of Tutsis fought pitched battles alongside the Congolese insurgents of the People's Liberation Army (APL) against the Congo National Army in South Kivu which was supported by the CIA and anti-Castro Cubans (recruited by the United States government), as well as by Belgium and South African white mercenaries.

The pro-Lumumba nationalist forces were backed by China, the Soviet Union, Cuba which sent Che Guevara and hundreds of troops, and by a number of African countries, especially Tanzania, Ghana, Egypt, Algeria, Guinea and Mali whose leaders – Nyerere, Nkrumah, Nasser, Ben Bella, Sekou Toure and Modibo Keita – constituted what was known within the Organisation of African Unity (OAU) as The Group of Six.

In an interview in Geneva, Switzerland, on 4 November 1995 with Jorge Castañeda, the author of *Compañero: The Life and Death of Che Guevara*, Ben Bella said the six leaders worked secretly among themselves on a number of African issues, excluding other African leaders. One of the most urgent subjects they dealt with during that period was the Congo crisis.

Recalling those days, Ben Bella said in the same interview: "We arrived in the Congo too late."

He was talking about the progressive African countries including his, Algeria, which intervened in Congo to help pro-Lumumbist forces.

One of those countries was Tanzania, Congo's neighbour, which, under Nyerere's leadership, served as a conduit for material assistance to Lumumba's followers fighting the puppet central government. Che Guevara and Cuban troops also went to Congo through Tanzania.

Tutsi guerrillas in eastern Congo were some of the most important players on the Congo scene during that turbulent period. While the Tutsi guerrillas played a

34

significant role in spreading the rebellion to the south and into northern Katanga Province together with the Congolese nationalist rebels, they also launched many cross-border raids into Rwanda in an attempt to destabilise and overthrow the Rwandan Hutu-dominated government.

As expected, those incursions, which failed to dislodge the Hutu from power, triggered a vicious retaliatory response by the Rwandan army and other Hutus against the Tutsi living in Rwanda; the majority of them still lived in Rwanda, their home country. Those who fled into exile constituted a minority of the Rwandan Tutsi population, although a significant one.

Thirty years later, the Hutu genocidal murderers – known as Interahamwe, which means "those who kill together" – employed some of the same strategies and tactics to try and dislodge the Tutsi-dominated government of the Rwandan Patriotic Front (RPF) which ousted the Hutu regime in July 1994 and stopped the genocide. Again, like the Rwandan Tutsi refugees who fled to eastern Congo during the 1960s, the Hutu perpetrators of the 1994 Rwandan genocide also sought refuge in eastern Zaire (renamed Congo in May 1997), together with hundreds of thousands of other Hutus. They also used eastern Congo as their operational base from which they launched raids into Rwanda in an attempt to remove the Tutsi-dominated RPF government.

But there were also some differences between the two. Hundreds of Rwandan Tutsi refugees fought as guerrillas in the 1964 Congolese rebellion against the Congolese national government. In contrast to that, an even much larger force of tens of thousands – no fewer than 30,000 – of Hutu rebels (including the Interahamwe and remnants of the defeated Hutu army who also sought refuge in eastern Zaire after losing to the Rwandan Patriotic Army (RPA) of the RPF in Rwanda) were actively involved in the insurgency against the Tutsi-dominated Rwandan government. The insurgency was launched in 1995 from the Hutu refugee camps in eastern Zaire and went on for years.

The Hutu rebels operating from eastern Zaire during the 1990s and thereafter also had perfect cover, hiding and moving freely among their kinsmen in the refugee camps. The Rwandan Tutsis launching cross-border raids against the Hutu regime in the sixties had no such sanctuary in eastern Congo.

The Hutu insurgents also controlled the refugee camps. And President Mobutu Sese Seko of Zaire, who was hostile to the Tutsi regimes in both Rwanda and Burundi – he was also hostile to the Ugandan government of President Yoweri Museveni – supplied the Hutu rebels with a lot of weapons and ammunition which they used to wage war against the Rwandan government, dominated by Tutsis, making them an even bigger threat to Rwanda's and even to Burundi's security.

And unlike in 1964 when there was a rebellion in eastern Congo which some of the Rwandan Tutsi refugees joined, there was no such uprising in eastern Zaire in 1995 when the Rwandan Hutu rebels launched their first raid into Rwanda. When one started in October – November 1996, it was with the full support of the Tutsi Rwandan army in order to destroy the perpetrators of the 1994 genocide – the Interahamwe and the remnants of the Hutu Rwandan Armed Forces (FAR) – and oust their ally, Mobutu Sese Seko, from power. The rebellion was also under Rwandan control.

The 1996 rebellion was launched and spearheaded by the Tutsi in eastern Zaire against Mobutu's regime which stripped them of their citizenship in 1981 – and in fact insisted that they had never even been citizens before then. But when it gained momentum rolling across the country towards the capital Kinshasa to oust Mobutu, it was Tutsi army officers from the Rwandan national army who provided the leadership; with Laurent Kabila, anointed by Rwanda's *de facto* ruler Paul Kagame, as the nominal head of the rebellion.

The 1996 – 1997 Congolese (Zairean) insurgency succeeded in ousting the central government, while the 1964 insurrection fail to accomplish the same objective.

After the end of the Cold War, Mobutu became an expendable commodity. He was no longer seen by the United States as an asset; it was the Americans and their allies who installed him in power to use him in their struggle to contain Soviet expansionism in Africa.

By contrast, the pro-Lumumbist forces failed to dislodge him from power during the sixties for exactly the opposite reason. The West saw Mobutu as an indispensable ally against the Soviet Union right in the heart of Africa where the Soviets and their satellites in the Eastern bloc, including the anti-Soviet and anti-West People's Republic of China, were trying to gain a foothold. And both the Congolese nationalist rebels and their Rwandan Tutsi allies in the 1964 uprising were regarded by the United States and other Western powers as the vanguard of communist penetration into the heart of the African continent.

That was one of the reasons why the CIA actively intervened to neutralise the insurgency. And it succeeded in doing so.

But the main reason for the intervention – even if the Soviet Union and China had never existed – was continued domination and exploitation of Africa the United States and other Western countries, especially the former colonial powers, saw as their sphere of influence they had been entitled to since the advent of colonial rule.

Although the two rebellions – in 1964 and 1996 – had little in common in terms of ideology and objectives besides the desire to overthrow the central government even if for different reasons, they had one thing in common: Tutsi involvement. The Tutsi played a major role in both uprisings. They also had one actor on the political scene who provided a historical link between them. And that was Laurent Kabila.

Before he became the leader of the Alliance of Democratic Forces for the Liberation of Congo-Zaire (ADFL) which ousted Mobutu from power, Kabila had been active at different times in the Fizi-Baraka area along Lake Tanganyika in eastern Zaire as the head of a small group – a continuation from the sixties' pro-Lumumbist rebellion – fighting to overthrow the regal autocrat, Mobutu, who rose to power with the help of the CIA. In fact, during his tenure as president of Zaire for 32 years, the largest CIA station in Africa was in Kinshasa.

But the group Kabila led in the Fizi-Baraka area was handicapped by its ethnic base, small membership, diminishing revolutionary stature, and by its inability to wage war even against the decaying Zairean state which had only a rag-tag army incapable of defending the country.

Kabila's group further compromised whatever stature and status it had when its members kidnapped four American students from Stanford University doing research in Kigoma Region in western Tanzania, across Lake Tanganyika from the rebel base on the lake's western shore in Zaire. They took them across the lake to their base in Zaire. As Professor Crawford Young stated in "Zaire: The Unending Crisis," in *Foreign Affairs*:

"One insurgent movement within the country lingers from the 1964 – 65 wave of rebellions.

Localized in the Fizi-Baraka area by Lake Tanganyika, this group – known in recent years as the *Parti de la Révolution Populaire* (PRP) – achieved notoriety in 1975 by kidnapping four Stanford students from a zoological research station in Tanzania.

Its composition is ethnically restricted to Bembe, though its leader, Laurent Kabila, is a Shaba (formerly Katanga) Luba.

The movement now has only a few hundred followers,

38

and has no possibility of enlarging its base of operations."[12]

Kabila himself had lost some credibility because of his frequent long absences from his operational base in eastern Zaire preferring, instead, to live in Dar es Salaam, Tanzania's capital, which became his home for more than 20 years.

Even his revolutionary credentials during the 1960s were questionable. He did not spend as much time in Congo as he should have, leaving his soldiers alone. As Che Guevara, who went to Congo to help the guerrillas, stated about Kabila's leadership: "I always thought that he did not have enough military experience; he was an agitator who had the stuff of a leader, yet lacked seriousness, aplomb, knowledge, in short this innate talent that one senses in Fidel the minute you meet him."[13] And as Che stated in another assessment of Kabila and the other Congolese rebel leaders including Soumialot in his letter from the shores of Lake Tanganyika in eastern Congo to Fidel Castro in October 1965:

"Sumialot and his companions have sold you an enormous bridge. It would take us forever to enumerate the huge number of lies they told you....I know Kabila well enough to have no illusions in his regard....

I have some background on Sumialot, like for example the lies he told you, the fact that he has not set foot on this godforsaken land, his frequent drinking bouts in Dar-es-Salaam, where he stays in the best hotels....

They are given huge amounts of money, all at once, to live splendidly in every African capital, not to mention that they are housed by the main progressive countries who often finance their travel expenses....The scotch and the women are also covered by friendly governments and if one likes good scotch and beautiful women, that costs a lot of money."[14]

When Che Guevara sent the letter to Castro, the Congolese rebel leaders had just been received in Havana, Cuba, like true revolutionaries and were treated with great respect, with Castro and other Cuban leaders who were backing them, unaware of their true characters.

Thirty years later during the the 1996 – 1997 rebellion which finally toppled Mobutu, most people still did not know much about Kabila. He had just been plucked out of obscurity and made the leader of the insurgency, riding on a wave of anti-Mobutu sentiments prevalent across the nation. He also had one major asset in a rebel movement whose driving force was Tutsi, an ethnic group hated not only in eastern Zaire where the rebellion started in 1996, but also in the rest of the country. He was not a Tutsi.

He was a member of the Luba tribe from northern Shaba Province (the former Katanga Province), an ethnic group accepted by the other tribes in Congo as native to the country unlike the Tutsi who were considered to be foreigners in spite of the fact that they have lived in Congo for more than 200 years. The Luba are also one of the largest ethnic groups in Congo.

Kabila's stature among his fellow countrymen, after Rwanda's *de facto* ruler General Paul Kagame chose him to lead the 1996 uprising against Mobutu, was enhanced by his own revolutionary credentials during the 1960s, however dubious those credentials were; by his political base as head of the small but resilient Afro-Marxist People's Revolutionary Party he founded in northern Katanga Province in 1967 which was now based in the Fizi-Baraka area on the western shore of Lake Tanganyika in South Kivu Province; and by his virulently anti-Mobutist stand as well as his credentials as a disciple of Patrice Lumumba.

But all those advantages were not enough to form a solid foundation on which to build a cohesive anti-Mobutist alliance.

The Anti-Mobutu Coalition

As we learned earlier, the fighting in eastern Zaire started in October – November 1996.

That was when Mobutu's rag-tag army and members of different tribes made a move against the Banyamulenge Tutsis – so named because of the mountainous Mulenge area in which they settled in South Kivu Province – whom they did not consider to be citizens.

The Banyamulenge fought back to protect their rights, especially the land which their enemies wanted to seize and force them to flee to Rwanda and Burundi to live with their fellow Tutsis.

Opposition to Mobutu's brutal kleptocratic rule by different groups in and out of Zaire led to the convening of a national conference in 1991 in the capital Kinshasa to address the nation's problems across the spectrum. After 30 years of chaos, anarchy and dictatorship during which all institutions of civic organisation and democratic tradition collapsed and were pulverised by the vampire state, the conference was willing to discuss any political or social problems facing the nation.

Such frank discussion was undoubtedly democratic. But it also had potential for catastrophe in the context of Zaire's toxic ethno-regional politics, given the intense tribal hostilities in some parts of the country, especially in North and South Kivu provinces.

The delegates from Kivu competed against each other as they articulated conflicting ethnic interests, each tribe promoting its own. But they agreed on one thing: the Tutsi had to go.

It was, however, a broad agenda, calling for the neutralisation of all Kinyarwanda speakers (hence Hutus as well) – Kinyarwanda is the national language of Rwanda spoken by Hutus and Tutsis – in the two Kivu provinces and, as a final solution, possibly their expulsion from Zaire, forcing them to "go back" where they "came from," Rwanda, a place most of them had never been to, and which they knew about only from historical ties.

But the primary target of the campaign was the Tutsi, citizens of Zaire, yet not "citizens." They were not considered to be citizens even by the national government of Mobutu, let alone by their fellow countrymen.

Although their migration from Rwanda to what came to be known as Congo started in the 16th century when King Kigeri Nyamuheshera sent a number of Tutsi families to settle in the newly conquered area of Bunyabungo in what is Uvira today in South Kivu Province in the eastern part of the country, it was the latter migrations – including the second and third waves in the 1800s – which drew more attention because of their cumulative impact.

Others followed, and a larger part of them, including the previous ones, settled mainly in what is now North Kivu Province across the border from Rwanda. As Gérard Prunier stated in "The Great Lakes Crisis":

"There were many layers of Rwandan immigration in eastern Zaire, especially in North Kivu.

The first group of Rwandans had arrived there probably over 200 years ago. These were both Tutsi and Hutu.

Many – mostly Hutu – were later 'imported' by the Belgians, who were short of manpower in the Congo during the colonial years while their mandate territory of Ruanda-Urundi (now Rwanda and Burundi) was overpopulated....

Rwanda and Burundi were parts of German East Africa (Tanganyika which is now Tanzania); they were conquered by the Belgian army in 1916 and later given to Brussels as mandate territories by the League of Nations....

A third and purely Tutsi layer was made up of refugees

42

who had fled the 1959 to 1963 massacres and the imposition of a Hutu ethnic state at the time of Rwanda's independence in 1962. And a fourth and exclusively Hutu group had arrived in August 1994, fleeing the RPF (the Tutsi Rwandan Patriotic Front) takeover in Rwanda."[15]

Delegates to the 1991 national conference in Kinshasa resorted to a legal manoeuvre to strip the Banyarwanda of their citizenship by selective implementation of citizenship laws to enforce the 1981 decree which revoked their status as citizens of Zaire.

President Mobutu himself supported the move by the delegates which helped divert some attention from his rotten dictatorship by mobilising nationalist sentiment against these "foreigners."

It was a tactic typical of Mobutu: divide and rule.

Earlier, he had used the Banyarwanda in Kivu provinces to help contain and neutralise local opposition to his rule from other tribes. It was one of the reasons why these ethnic groups became even more hostile towards the Banyarwanda (mostly Tutsis) and towards Mobutu himself.

Members of these tribes in eastern Zaire proceeded to disenfranchise "outsiders" by launching a campaign of ethnic cleansing.

The campaign had a broad mandate – to expel all non-indigenes including non-Banyarwanda – but was specific in intent, and selective in its application, by targeting the Banyarwanda.

By early 1993, tribal militia groups were ransacking villages and killing the Banyarwanda in North Kivu Province which borders Rwanda. The victims included Hutus but the primary target was Tutsis because of the intense hostility towards them by the local tribes and other Zaireans.

In the past, the Tutsi and the Hutu in Congo had, collectively as Banyarwanda, formed a united front against their common enemy: the other tribes in eastern Congo who did not want them there. But with the civil war in Rwanda between their kinsmen, Hutu versus Tutsi, they also turned against each other in Congo (Zaire). No longer were they fellow Banyarwanda, with a shared identity based on common national origin, Rwanda; they were simply Hutus and Tutsis. Each to his own.

In 1993, North Kivu became a battleground and witnessed some of the most violent conflicts between different tribes in recent times. Hutus fought Tutsis, and vice versa; and members of the other tribes fought both.

The influx of the Hutu Rwandan refugees into the region in mid-1994, fleeing from Rwanda after the Tutsi-dominated Rwandan Patriotic Front (RPF) took over the country and stopped the genocide of Tutsis, aggravated the situation.

Among the Hutu refugees were tens of thousands of well-armed and virulently anti-Tutsi elements who had participated in the massacre of almost one million Tutsis in Rwanda during the 1994 genocide.

The result was ethnic cleansing in eastern Zaire reminiscent of what had just taken place across the border in Rwanda. Thousands of Tutsis were killed, and the rest fled to Rwanda where the Tutsi-led Rwandan Patriotic Front had just seized power.

The ethnic conflict had overflown national boundaries with dire consequences, adding a new dimension to the genocide against the Tutsi.

The situation in South Kivu Province was somewhat different. Like their counterparts in North Kivu Province, the leaders of South Kivu had also decided to disenfranchise the Banyarwanda. However, the division between the Hutu and the Tutsi was not as pronounced as it was in North Kivu.

The Banyarwanda who had settled in this region (South Kivu) are the ones who were named Banyamulenge by the members of the other tribes in the region. They

44

were mostly Tutsi who settled in the area in the early 1800s after losing in intra-tribal feudal wars with fellow Tutsis in Rwanda. They were accompanied by their Hutu servants who became assimilated into the larger Tutsi community, "losing" their Hutu identity in the process. Like their Tutsi masters, they simply came to be known as Banyamulenge, or just "Tutsis."

In 1993 and 1994, the Banyamulenge witnessed with horror the ethnic cleansing of fellow Tutsis in North Kivu Province and prepared for the worst. By mid-1996, when provincial leaders of South Kivu with the full support of the central government in Kinshasa began to target them, they decided to take decisive action. And they got immediate help from Rwanda where their kinsmen were now in control.

They also sought help from Burundi, which was under under Tutsi leadership like Rwanda, and from Uganda whose president, Kaguta Yoweri Museveni, was himself identified as a Tutsi, although he identified himself as a Munyankole, a member of the Banyankole ethnic group in southwestern Uganda who are related to the Tutsi.

But among all their supporters, it was Rwanda, their original homeland, which was their patron.

By November 1996, eastern Zaire was engulfed in civil war. As the fighting intensified between the Banyamulenge Tutsis and the Zairean army with its anti-Tutsi local supporters, the Tutsi won the support of other Zairean opposition groups which wanted to oust Mobutu from power. It was a marriage of convenience. According to *Africa Analysis*:

"[The opposition groups include] the Popular Revolutionary Party of Shaba Province, the Revolutionary Liberation Movement and the National Democratic Resistance from the Kasai region.

These have now joined the Banyamurenge to form an umbrella organisation, the Alliance of Democratic

45

Liberation Forces of Zaire and Congo.

It aims to oust the ailing President Mobutu Sese Seko from power. Even more ominously, Rwandan troops have reportedly joined the fighting. Zaire claims some fighters captured in the country belong to Rwanda's 7th infantry battalion and also accuses Ugandan and Burundian forces of aiding the rebels."[16]

Other countries besides Rwanda which joined the anti-Mobutu coalition included Angola, Tanzania, Eritrea, Ethiopia, Zimbabwe, and Zambia.

The Banyamulenge, whose oppression ignited the rebellion, were no longer an isolated group in their campaign against Mobutu.

Ironically, in the late 1960s when Pierre Mulele led Congo's longest uprising, the "Kwilu" rebellion from his operational base in his home Kwilu Province in the western part of the country, it was the Banyamulenge who helped Mobutu fight the pro-Lumumbist rebels.

It was he who first armed them with modern weapons, enthusiastically embracing them as fellow Congolese in his hour of need. Before then, the Banyamulenge had depended on bows and arrows.

Thirty years later, they switched sides and fought to overthrow the very same man they once helped to keep in power. They also formed an alliance with the pro-Lumumbist forces of Laurent Kabila, the same forces they fought thirty years before, helping Mobutu to neutralise them.

The advance by the insurgents across Zaire during the 1996 – 1997 rebellion was directed by the military leaderships of Rwanda, Uganda, and Burundi. And there was evidence from the beginning showing that Rwanda had been arming the Banyamulenge in the same way that Uganda had armed the Rwandan Patriotic Front (RPF) fighters who went on to seize power in Kigali, Rwanda's capital. In fact, Rwanda's ruler Paul Kagame conceded later that the war was planned primarily by Rwanda, and that the plan to topple Mobutu also originated in Kigali.

He disclosed in an interview with *The Washington Post*, 9 July 1997, that "the Rwandan government planned and directed the rebellion that ousted the long-time dictator and that Rwandan troops and officers led the rebel forces."[17]

The prominent role played by the Banyamulenge in overthrowing Mobutu in May 1997 was deeply resented by the members of the other tribes in eastern Zaire where the rebellion started. Those with deep resentment included the Babembe, the Bahunda, the Banande, and the Bashi. The Banyamulenge were also resented by others across the country, including the Baluba, Laurent Kabila's tribe in Shaba (Katanga) Province.

The resentment got even deeper when several Banyamulenge Tutsis assumed key positions in the national government in Kinshasa under President Laurent Kabila who was seen by many of his fellow countrymen as a puppet of Rwanda, and their giant nation a virtual colony of their tiny neighbour: Rwanda. And the contrast is glaring. Congo which is the size of Western Europe or the entire United States of America east of the Mississippi River is about 90 times the size of Rwanda.

And the role played by Rwanda, Uganda, and Burundi in overthrowing Mobutu and in installing a new government in Kinshasa raised speculation of a concerted effort by the leaders of the three countries to create a Tutsi empire in East-Central Africa, from the Great Lakes region to the Atlantic Ocean.

Rwanda and Burundi were clearly Tutsi-dominated states. In the case of Uganda, Tutsi leadership of that country centred on President Kaguta Yoweri Museveni, a member of the Hima branch of the Tutsi from the southwestern part of Uganda bordering Rwanda and Tanzania. Also, there were those who contended that Museveni was actually a Tutsi from Rwanda. And they have maintained the same position through the years.

Expansionist ambitions of the three countries could not be ruled out. And they were directed at Congo ostensibly for security reasons to secure the borders of those countries against incursions by rebel groups based in Congo who were trying to overthrow the governments of the three countries.

But even if they had territorial ambitions to annex parts of Congo, directly or indirectly, there is no question that security of their borders also figured prominently in their decision to intervene in Congo.

Of the three countries, Rwanda was most vulnerable because of the tens of thousands of armed Hutu extremists – including members of the former Hutu Rwandan national army who were defeated by the Rwandan Patriotic Army (RPA) of the RPF in 1994 – who had fled the country after the Rwandan genocide and found sanctuary just across the border in Congo. But whether or not such concern about security was of paramount importance, eclipsing everything else, in Rwanda's intervention in Congo is a matter for argument.

Rwanda's Strategic Initiatives in Congo

Rwanda intervened in Congo for several reasons and in a vengeful mood: to kill, indiscriminately, hundreds of thousands of Hutu refugees – including innocent men, women and children and the elderly – in retaliation for the 1994 genocide in which one million Tutsis perished at the hands of Hutu extremists and, in fact, succeeded in massacring more than 200,000 of those refugees in only a few months.

Rwandan Tutsi leaders also intervened in Congo to hunt down the perpetrators of the 1994 genocide who were hiding among the refugees in refugee camps, making it almost impossible to identify them when they were mixed with other people in the camps. To kill them, Rwandan Tutsi soldiers also had to kill innocent Hutu refugees, virtually sparing none, to make sure the perpetrators of the genocide hiding among them were dead.

Rwanda also went into Congo to install a puppet regime in Kinshasa it could manipulate at will in pursuit of its national interests; to secure its borders by any means at its disposal; to create a buffer zone, in effect, a *de facto* autonomous state inhabited by Congolese Tutsis, along the Rwandan-Congolese border ostensibly as a security measure but in fact as an expansionist move to create a Tutsi federation or confederation of the two Tutsi political entities: Rwanda and the newly created Tutsi state in the "security corridor."

Rwanda also intervened in Congo for economic reasons: to extract Congo's mineral resources and agricultural products, including gold, diamonds, coffee, and timber; and if possible, to annex parts of eastern Congo in pursuit of its hegemonic ambitions in East-Central Africa as a power broker in the region despite its small size. Rwanda is one of the smallest countries in Africa and in the entire world, yet one of the most influential in the Great Lakes region of East-Central Africa.

But foremost among all those objectives was security for this tiny, highly vulnerable, desperately poor and landlocked nation in the hinterland of Africa. Even its expansionist ambition may be justified by the "imperial" authorities in Kigali in terms of security concerns, although it can not be defended on rational grounds. Rwanda's security can not be guaranteed in Congo but in Rwanda itself, especially by treating all its citizens equally without discrimination across the spectrum.

Yet there were grounds for such intervention in Congo by Rwanda.

The immediate cause of Rwanda's intervention was the persecution of the Banyamulenge Tutsi in eastern Congo –

then known as Zaire – by the other tribes in South Kivu Province; a persecution which led to armed conflict in August 1996 between the Banyamulenge and the other ethnic groups supported by Mobutu's national army.

It was, at first, seen as a local conflict. But it assumed larger dimensions when it became clear that the two Tutsi-dominated states of Rwanda and Burundi intervened to help their kinsmen.

The conflict escalated even further when Uganda intervened in November 1996, forming a tripartite alliance with Rwanda and Burundi which went on to overthrow Mobutu and later plunge Congo into a much bigger war involving armies from nine African countries.

All three – Rwanda, Burundi and Uganda – intervened in eastern Zaire ostensibly to secure their borders because Mobutu's government was harbouring rebel groups fighting to overthrow their governments. Yet the threat to Uganda was not as serious as the Ugandan authorities claimed it was.

It came mainly from northern and northwestern Uganda where the West Nile Bank Liberation Front, linked to the remnants of Idi Amin's regime, and the Lord's Resistance Army (LRA), were operating.

The Lord's Resistance Army was made up of members of the Holy Spirit Movement, a millenarian cult mostly composed of Acholi tribesmen indigenous to northern Uganda.

Both groups were armed by the Sudanese government in retaliation for Uganda's support of the black African rebels of the Sudanese People's Liberation Army (SPLA) in southern Sudan fighting against the Arab-dominated government in Khartoum in pursuit of autonomy and ultimately independence. And both had operational bases in Zaire, in addition to those in Sudan, and within Uganda itself.

But neither posed a serious threat to the Ugandan government because they operated mainly in northern

Uganda far from the capital Kampala which is in the south. Also, both groups were weak. And they were severely compromised by their ethnic appeal in the region – northern Uganda – which is ethnically heterogeneous, a diversity which made it very difficult, if not impossible, for them to broaden their support.

The threat to Burundi from the Hutu rebels operating from Zaire, although very serious, was not enough to oust the government because of the entrenched Tutsi ethnocracy which had consolidated its power since independence in 1962 by systematically destroying the Hutu elite and massacring hundreds of thousands of Hutus through the years.

Its firm grip on power is attested to by the fact that Burundi's capital, Bujumbura, is only 10 miles from the border with the Democratic Republic of Congo, formerly Zaire. Yet, in spite of such proximity making Burundi even more vulnerable to attack, Burundian Hutu rebels operating from their bases in Congo and within Burundi itself have not been able to threaten the capital seriously, let alone oust the Tutsi from power.

The situation was different in Rwanda by mid-1996 when the regime in Kigali intervened in Zaire.

Devastated by the 1994 holocaust, the country was still in a daze. The economy was in ruins, and institutions of governance and civic organisation had also been destroyed.

The victorious Rwandan Patriotic Front (RPF) – which ousted and replaced the genocidal Hutu regime and assumed power as Rwanda's "legitimate" government although without electoral mandate – was mostly Tutsi and therefore not trusted by the Hutu majority who were excluded from the government in terms of meaningful representation besides token leadership.

And the new Tutsi rulers knew that they could not trust most Hutus – who also constitute the vast majority of the population – because there was no guarantee that they disassociated themselves from or turned their backs on the perpetrators of the 1994 genocide.

Distrust of the new Tutsi rulers among the Hutu deepened when Prime Minister Faustin Twagiramungu and Interior Minister Seth Sendashonga, both Hutus, were forced to resign in August 1995. The remaining Hutu government ministers were also forced out shortly thereafter, leaving the RPF regime, already Tutsi-dominated, ethnically isolated, despite its earlier promises to form an inclusive government.

Such politics of exclusion could guarantee only one thing: perpetual conflict between the two groups. And that is exactly what happened during the following years.

Compounding the problem for the Tutsi-dominated government was the fact that more than 2 million Rwandan Hutu refugees, many of whom – if not the majority – were hostile to the new rulers and other Tutsis in Rwanda, had found refuge just across the border in eastern Zaire and western Tanzania.

Among them were 50,000 soldiers of the former Hutu-dominated Rwandan Armed Forces (FAR), routed by the predominantly Tutsi Rwandan Patriotic Front (RPF) in July 1994. They were Hutu and most of them were camped in Zaire together with civilian Hutu refugees. And they were in the process of rearming themselves in the refugee camps and getting ready to invade Rwanda.

It was in this context that Rwanda decided to act. Its intervention to protect the Banyamulenge in eastern Zaire was indeed a prime motive. But it was linked to the greater security concerns of Rwanda, important as ethnic solidarity was.

Therefore even if there had been no Tutsis – the Banyamuluenge – who were being persecuted in Zaire, the Tutsi-dominated government of Rwanda would have intervened, anyway, to go after the perpetrators of the 1994 genocide who were hiding among the rest of the Hutu refugees in the refugee camps in eastern Zaire and who were preparing to invade Rwanda and oust the Tutsi from power.

The Rwandan government also intervened in Zaire out of malicious vindictiveness to exact retribution for the extermination of about one million Tutsis during the Rwandan genocide by massacring hundreds of thousands of Hutus, including women and children, who had sought refuge in Zaire.

The distrust and hatred between the two sides was mutual.

Hutu rebels were already launching raids into Rwanda from their bases in Zaire, killing and planting mines and trying to destabilise the Tutsi-dominated government before the Rwandan authorities intervened in Zaire. President Mobutu supplied them with weapons. He also gave them a lot of money. He hated the Tutsi regime in Rwanda which he also derisively dismissed as a puppet of Ugandan President Yoweri Museveni, his nemesis.

But even if Mobutu had wanted to restrain the rebels, he probably would not have been able to do so. The best he could have done would have been to deny them assistance, money and weapons, thus limiting their capability to attack Rwanda.

The Zairean state over which he presided was no more than an empty shell, crumbling and falling apart, pulverised from within due to neglect during his 30 years in office. Yet Zaire was potentially one of the richest countries in the world, in fact richer than South Africa in terms of mineral wealth. And the national army itself, the Zairian Armed Forces (FAZ), was in disarray and in tatters. It was no more than a rag-tag army of thugs, undisciplined, poorly trained, and underpaid solders who survived on robbery and looting, to pay themselves.

The Hutu rebels in Zaire were a formidable force, not only impossible to dislodge, but constantly replenished with weapons. They were also well-funded by other patrons besides Mobutu.

In addition to the weapons and ammunition they took when they fled Rwanda in 1994 and the supplies they got from President Mobutu, these former members of the Hutu Rwandan national army and the country's political leaders who were also among the refugees in Zaire or lived elsewhere while supporting the rebels had also looted Rwanda's national treasury when they fled their homeland.

They used the money to buy more weapons on the international black market, especially from the People's Republic of China, a country which also had a history of meddling in the Hutu-Tutsi ethnic conflicts since the early 1960s when it first intervened in both Rwanda and Burundi.

Towards the end of 1995 and in early 1996, Hutu incursions into Rwanda had escalated to the point where they posed a serious threat to the nation's security. But the attacks also triggered a brutal retaliatory response from the Tutsi Rwandan national army directed against Hutu civilians in Rwanda, most of whom were poor peasants living in villages across the country.

Such indiscriminate violence and brutal tactics, which amounted to state-sponsored terror, against the Hutu peasants probably the majority of whom were innocent, only aggravated the situation in a country where relations between the two ethnic groups were already bad. It also helped the Hutu rebels recruit even more fighters, driven into the rebels' arms by the terror campaign conducted by the Tutsi army against Hutu civilians.

The decision by many Hutus to join the rebels was understandable. It is only when you are in another man's condition that you may be able to understand his predicament. As Ehud Barak confessed in 1999 before being elected prime minister of Israel, had he been born a Palestinian, he would have joined the Palestine Liberation Organisation (PLO).[18]

Had the Tutsi been Hutus, they probably would be doing the same thing Hutu rebels are doing today.

However, that does not mean Rwanda under Tutsi leadership never had legitimate security concerns, as Hutu insurgents continued to launch cross-border raids into the country. For several months, Rwanda's ruler Paul Kagame had warned against such attacks from Zaire and complained that the refugee camps in Kivu provided cover for these rebels, enabling them to attack Rwanda with impunity.

He asked the international community to intervene and stop such subversive activities in the camps which had been set up with UN assistance and were under UN supervision. But his plea went unheeded.

Yet he also knew that an invasion of the refugee camps by his army to neutralise the rebels would tarnish Rwanda's image – breaking international law was the least of his concerns as he clearly demonstrated when he invaded Zaire shortly thereafter – by killing innocent civilians without even eliminating the threat from the insurgents hiding among them.

However, this humanitarian concern was also later ignored by Kagame, as was international law about the sanctity of national borders, when he invaded Zaire shortly thereafter.

Yet pursuit of the rebels was justified, the rationale behind it reminiscent of what Tanzania did in 1979 in response to Idi Amin's invasion of her territory. Tanzania fought back and crossed the border in pursuit of the invaders and forced Amin to flee Uganda after the capital Kampla fell to Tanzanian and anti-Amin forces on 10 April. From Tanzania's standpoint, it was a matter of national security.

That was also the case with Rwanda whose leader, Kagame, was also a great admirer of Tanzanian president, Julius Nyerere and his doctrine of justified intervention in other countries – although he never explicitly said so – who authorised the counterattack against Idi Amin's forces when they invaded Tanzania in October 1978 and annexed

55

710 square miles of her territory in Kagera Region in the northwestern part of the country bordering Uganda.

Of paramount importance was Rwanda's security when the Rwandan army intervened in Congo. As Kagame himself stated in an interview with *The Washington Post*, 9 July 1997:

"They were insensitive. We told them (the United Nations and world powers) that either they do something about the camps or they face the consequences."[19]

It was time to intervene. The Tutsi Rwandan Patriotic Front Army (RPA) then began training fellow Tutsis, the Banyamulenge, who went to Rwanda for the training, and also established contacts with other groups in Zaire opposed to Mobutu's regime in order to form a united front against one of Africa's most notorious tyrants.

On 18 October 1996, the opposition groups joined forces with the Banyamulenge Tutsis and formed the Alliance of Democratic Forces for the Liberation of Congo-Zaire (ADFL). The ADFL included four main anti-Mobutu groups, divided by ideology, but united in their opposition against a common enemy. They were:

The People's Democratic Alliance whose French acronym was *Alliance Democratique des Peuples* (ADP) led by Deogratias Bugera, a Banyamulenge Tutsi; the National Resistance Council for Democracy (*Conseil National de Resistance pour la Democratie* – CNRD) founded in 1993 by Andre Kisase Ngandu of the National Congolese Movement (*Mouvement National Congolais* – MNC/Lumumba); the Revolutionary Movement for the Liberation of Zaire (*Mouvement Revolutionnaire pour la Liberation du Zaire* – MRLZ) led by Masasu Nindaga; and the People's Revolutionary Party (*Parti de la Revolution Populaire* – PRP) led by Laurent-Desire Kabila who went on to become head of the anti-Mobutu coalition.

In early October 1996, Rwanda learned that the Hutu

rebels in Zaire were going to attack the Banyamulenge. Rwandan leaders also learned that the insurgents planned to invade Rwanda with about 100,000 Hutus including 40,000 militiamen.

The threat triggered a joint response from the Rwandan Tutsis and their Congolese kinsmen, the Banyamulenge.

After repeated attacks by Mobutu's soldiers and their local allies (members of tribes including Hutus hostile to the Tutsi), the Banyamulenge fought back. And they won. After routing Mobutu's rag-tag army, they attacked the Hutu refugee camps in eastern Zaire, triggering a mass exodus of hundreds of thousands of Hutus who returned to Rwanda. Hundreds of thousands of others fled west, deeper into the Congo forest, where at least 300,000 of them perished in addition to the 200,000 killed by Tutsi soldiers. The rest fled to Burundi.

In addition to the Hutu threat from Zaire, Rwanda was also deeply concerned about the situation in Burundi, its twin in the south.

Burundi's neighbours had imposed an economic embargo on the country because of a Tutsi-led military coup by Major Pierre Buyoya who ousted constitutionally chosen Hutu President Sylvestre Ntibantunganya in July 1996.

Earlier, Buyoya also orchestrated the abortive attempt to overthrow the government in October 1993 in which President Melchior Ndadaye, a Hutu, was assassinated.

The Tutsi government in Rwanda worried that if the Tutsi lost power to the Hutu in Burundi as a result of economic sanctions and Hutu guerrilla attacks, the Rwandan Hutu rebels would be welcomed by their kinsmen in Burundi who would provide them with a major operational base from which they could launch raids into Rwanda. And if Burundi fell and came under Hutu leadership, it would be only a matter of time before Rwanda did, with the Tutsi government in Kigali collapsing under a combined massive military attack by the Hutu in both countries. In fact, Rwandan and Burundian Hutu rebels have been coordinating their attacks against the Tutsi in both countries for years.

There was also great concern among the Tutsi leaders and their kinsmen in Rwanda that should Burundi fall into Hutu hands, a massacre of genocidal proportions directed against the Tutsi in that country was a very strong possibility, and probably on a scale reminiscent of what happened in Rwanda in 1994, if not worse. To avert such a catastrophe, Rwanda would have to throw its gates wide open to save fellow Tutsis fleeing Burundi before being exterminated.

Some of Burundi's Tutsi leaders, for example former President Jean-Baptiste Bagaza, a hardliner, believed that Rwanda was the only country where fleeing Tutsis could expect to be welcomed, now that it was again under Tutsi leadership after the 1994 genocide.

But it is an assessment not borne out by facts. Rwanda is not the only country where Tutsis could expect to be welcomed if they had to flee Burundi.

Tens of thousands of Tutsi refugees, not just Hutus, from both Rwanda and Burundi, have been welcomed in Tanzania through the years. And tens of thousands of them have acquired Tanzanian citizenship.

They have also been given refuge by other African countries including Uganda. For example, it was from Uganda that the Tutsi Rwandan Patriotic Front (RPF) launched its first – although abortive – invasion of Rwanda on 1 October 1990, including its last and successful one from 8 April – 4 July 1994.

Kenya also has welcomed Tutsi refugees as much as it has Hutus.

But the mere prospect of a massive Tutsi exodus from Burundi, should the Tutsi be ousted from power in that country, was enough to be a matter of serious concern to the Tutsi leadership in neighbouring Rwanda. Such a huge influx would simply lead to another explosion in Rwanda,

58

with Hutus and Tutsis slaughtering each other while fighting over limited space and scarce resources, not even to mention the total collapse of the nation's already overburdened and fragile economy in such a small, desperately poor and overpopulated country.

Therefore, the survival of the Tutsi government in Burundi was seen by the Rwandan Tutsi leaders as critical to the survival of Rwanda itself as a Tutsi ethnocracy and as a safe haven for its dominant ethnic group.

So, it was not just a question of Tutsi ethnic solidarity with their kinsmen in Burundi which motivated the Rwandan leaders to help them stay in power, although ethnic loyalty to each other has always figured prominently in the calculations of both states. It was also a question of Rwanda's survival as a Tutsi ethnocracy, vital to the survival of the Tutsi as a people, that was at stake, as much as Burundi's survival under Tutsi domination was seen as critical to the survival of Tutsis in both countries bound by common destiny.

The Rwanda leaders felt that the threat to their country's security could be best dealt with by supporting the Banyamulenge in their war against their common enemies: the Hutu operating from Zaire, and President Mobutu and his local allies – different tribes – in the eastern part of the country who were equally hostile to the Tutsi in Zaire, Rwanda, and Burundi.

It is true that Rwanda's support for the Banyamulenge and other anti-Mobutist forces – who collectively constituted the Alliance of Democratic Forces for the Liberation of Congo-Zaire – led to the ouster of Mobutu. But it did not lead to the establishment of a friendly regime in Kinshasa – Kabila turned out to be only a temporary ally of convenience – or neutralise the threat to Rwanda's or Burundi's security coming from the Hutu rebels based in Congo.

Security of the two countries can be guaranteed only when the dominant Tutsi minority – in control of both

Rwanda and Burundi – agree to share power with the Hutu majority on the basis of a mutually acceptable compromise. And that includes proportional representation in the government and other areas of national life where power sharing is critical to the survival, wellbeing and prosperity of both groups.

Prospects for Peace

Prospects for a lasting peace in the Great Lakes region are bleak, to say the least. And that will continue to be the case as long as the leaders of Rwanda, Burundi and Congo remain adamantly opposed to devolution of power; and as long as different tribes continue to fight each other and dominate one another.

The twentieth century came to an end without any of the conflicts – in Rwanda, Burundi, Congo, and even in less troubled Uganda – being resolved.

Rwanda and Burundi remained mired in escalating ethnic warfare, with the Hutu vowing to overthrow the Tutsi, and the Tutsi refusing to share power with the Hutu except on their own terms.

Peace in Congo remained elusive even after a peace agreement was signed by all the countries and rebel groups involved in that multinational conflict.

And in Uganda, the government continued to fight its own rebels.

And despite professions to the contrary, Rwanda and Burundi continued to be ruled by quasi-military, not civilian, governments, as the twentieth-first century began; so did the Democratic Republic of Congo whose name is a misnomer in a country without democracy. And all three countries remained deeply divided along ethnic lines.

It is these ethnic rivalries, among other reasons, which African soldiers have always used to justify military coups, claiming that they are trying to inculcate a truly national ethos among the people, while at the same time they continue to maintain the status quo of tribal and regional loyalties. And it is the same ethnic hostilities which have helped to ignite and fuel civil wars in the Great Lakes region through the years in the struggle for power and resources among different groups.

Seizure of power by the military has proved to be the fastest and probably most effective means to achieve this goal, of tribal supremacy, but with dire consequences for the countries involved as the history of military rule in Africa tragically demonstrates.

Military rule has led to institutionalised ethnocracy: for example, by the Kabye in Togo where President Gnassingbe Eyadema, Africa's longest-ruling autocrat in power since 1967, virtually excluded the country's largest ethnic group, the Ewe, and members of other tribes from power and filled the army with members of his tribe – more than two-thirds of the soldiers and army officers were Kabye – from northern Togo; by the Amhara in Ethiopia where Mengistu Haile Mariam seized power in 1977, perpetuating Amharic rule which had gone on for years even before him; by the Tutsi in both Rwanda and Burundi; and by the Hutu in Rwanda since independence in 1962 until they were ousted from power following the 1994 genocide.

Military rule has also led to entrenchment of dictatorship and institutionalisation of corruption as a national virtue, as has been the case under civilian leadership in most African countries. There are many case studies which document this abuse of power across the continent,[20] as the history of military and civilian rule in Africa clearly shows.

Rwanda and Burundi are some of the best case studies of military and civilian dictatorship in Africa whose tyranny plunged the two countries into full-scale civil wars. They also have been the scene of some of the bloodiest conflicts on the continent in the post-colonial period.

Part Two:

Burundi: A Nation at War

THE African continent has been the scene of many tragedies through the years. But few equal what happened in Rwanda and Burundi in terms of Africans killing fellow Africans. Rwanda and Burundi easily qualify as the killing fields of Africa, two countries of magnificent beauty, with green hills and valleys, soaked in blood.

Even Nigeria's tragedy during the civil war from 1967 to 1970 pales into insignificance by comparison in terms of the number of victims and the magnitude of the violence unleashed.

This is not to ignore the suffering of the Igbos and other Eastern Nigerians in that war. It was a horrendous tragedy. But Northern Nigerians did not slaughter hundreds of thousands of Igbos and other Easterners in Northern Nigeria as the Hutu and the Tutsi did to each other in Rwanda and Burundi from the early sixties to the mid-nineties alone.

Most of the victims during that tragic period in Nigerian – and African – history died from starvation, a weapon the federal military government deliberately used effectively to starve the Igbos and other Eastern Nigerians into submission. As Chief Anthony Enahoro, the commissioner of information in the Nigerian government under General Yakubu Gowon, bluntly stated at a press conference in July 1968: "Starvation is a legitimate instrument of war, and we have every intention of using it against the rebels."

Chief Obafemi Awolowo, vice chairman of the Federal Executive Council, hence Nigeria's vice president under Gowon who was the head of the federal military government, articulated the same position.

In Rwanda and Burundi, most of the victims were simply slaughtered – hacked, clubbed, stoned, slashed, speared or shot to death. And the carnage continues today.

Although this chapter is about Burundi, it is also about Rwanda because the two countries have so much in common that they literally constitute one country, had it not been for the demarcation line that separates them. At the very least, they are identical twins. The artificial boundary has not changed that. Yet, both are so divided within that each is, tragically, two nations in one, hence four in both: Hutu versus Tutsi.

Formerly known as Ruanda-Urundi, the two countries were a part of what is Tanzania today when all three formed one country called German East Africa (Deutsch-Ostafrika).

The area that came to be known as Tanganyika, what is now Tanzania mainland, is the country that was first named Deutsch Ostafrika (German East Africa). Burundi, then known as Urundi, became part of German East Africa in 1898, and Rwanda, then called Ruanda, in 1899.

After Germany was defeated in World War I, both Ruanda and Urundi were mandated to Belgium by the League of Nations as one territory of Ruanda-Urundi. The territory was administered jointly with Belgian Congo. The administrative centre was Leopoldville, the capital of Belgian Congo which was renamed Kinshasa by President Mobutu in 1966.

Tanganyika, which was the largest part of the East African German colony, became a British mandated territory after Woodrow Wilson, the American president, turned down a request by British Prime Minister Lloyd George to administer it under the League of Nations trusteeship mandate. Otherwise Tanganyika, what is mainland Tanzania today, would have become an American colony or possession, the only one on the continent. Liberia is considered by some people to be a virtual American colony; some even consider it to be America's 51st state. But that is an entirely different subject beyond the scope of this work.

Had the three territories – of Tanganyika, Ruanda and Urundi – remained together and emerged from colonial rule as a single political entity, the history of the Great Lakes region would probably have been different.

It is possible the massacres of the Hutu and the Tutsi which have taken place in both Rwanda and Burundi through the years, including the 1994 genocide, would not have taken place. It is also possible many Hutus and Tutsis would have moved to other parts of the large country – the former German East Africa – instead of remaining crowded in the heavily populated territories of Ruanda and Urundi fighting for scarce resources especially land.

It is also possible there would have been an equitable distribution of power in the larger political entity in which the Hutu and the Tutsi would not have been locked in conflict as they are now in Rwanda and Burundi.

The Hutu constitute the vast majority of Burundi's

population, a formidable 85 per cent, and the Tutsi, 14 per cent. The Twa, who are the Pygmies, make up the remaining 1 per cent.

But it is the Tutsi who have always dominated the country and the government. It is this inequity of power, probably more than anything else, which has caused so much bloodshed between the Hutu and the Tutsi through the years.

Other factors, especially shortage of land and poverty, have exacerbated the conflict.

Burundi is one of the poorest countries in the world. It is also the most densely populated country in Africa after Rwanda.

In such a small, desperately poor and overpopulated country, shortage of land may be the country's biggest problem. Had there been enough land, there would have been less conflict which has been an integral part of the country's history since the Tutsi conquered and virtually enslaved the Hutu about 400 years ago and established the kingdoms of Ruanda and Urundi under aristocratic rule.

Even after the end of colonial rule when it was expected that both the Hutu and the Tusti would equally participate in the government of their country, the asymmetrical relationship between the two ethnic groups continued. The Tutsi remained in a dominant position.

On 1 July 1962, the Tutsi-dominated kingdom of Urundi won independence as a monarchy. It was renamed Burundi under the leadership of Mwami (King) Mwambutsa IV.

But independence from Belgium did not usher in a new era of peace and stability for the country. The mid-sixties were marred by violence between the dominant Tutsis and the subjugated Hutus, and by struggle for power among the Tutsi themselves.

The assassination of Louis Rwagasore, a Tutsi and prominent nationalist, on 13 October 1961 by a Belgian just a few months before independence, exacerbated tensions ans intensified competition within the Tutsi elite in their quest for power, with different factions conniving against each other. The factionalism contributed to their defeat in the 1964 parliamentary elections which the Hutu won.

However, even without such intra-ethnic conflict among the Tutsi, the Hutu would probably have won the election, anyway, given their numerical preponderance if the elections were democratic, as they indeed were during the parliamentary contest.

Although the Hutu won the 1964 parliamentary elections, Burundi's head of state, Mwami (King) Mwambutsa IV, refused to appoint a Hutu prime minister to lead the cabinet. And that was at a time when the country was in a very tense political situation because of the intense hostility between the two ethnic groups.

Not long before the 1964 elections, fighting between the Hutu and the Tutsi erupted in December 1963 in which at least 5,000 people were killed following an invasion of Rwanda by Burundi-based Rwandan Tutsis with the help of their Burundian kinsmen in an attempt to overthrow the Hutu-dominated government of Rwanda.

Embittered by their exclusion from power as a result of King Mwambutsa's refusal to appoint a Hutu prime minister after an election they won, the Hutu tried to seize power from the Tutsi.

On 18 October 1965, Hutu insurgents in the Burundi army and gendarmerie in collusion with the Hutu elite and politicians attempted to assassinate Mwami Mwambutsa IV and the Tutsi prime minister he had appointed.

The coup was led by Gervais Nyangoma and succeeded deposing King Mwambutsa. Soon after the king was ousted, Hutus in the police force started killing Tutsis. The police force during that time was led by Antoine Serkwavu, a Hutu.

But the revolt did not last long and was violently suppressed by the Tutsi-dominated army and security forces.

The leader of the counter-coup was Michel Micombero, a Tutsi, who returned to Burundi during the same year after getting military training in Belgium. He had been quickly promoted after his return and was secretary of defence when King Mwambutsa was overthrown.

He mobilised forces in the army whose officers were mostly Tutsi and neutralised the Hutu who ousted the king. The king was reinstated.

Then a wave of violence was unleashed by the army and its Tutsi supporters against Hutus throughout the country.

At least 30 to 40 Hutu soldiers and gendarmes were summarily executed, sending a strong signal to the Hutu that any attempt to oust the Tutsi from power would be dealt with ruthlessly.

The executions were followed by a wave of violence that erupted in the hills above the capital, Bujumbura, formerly known as Usumbura, in which Hutu civilians joined fleeing gendarmes in burning Tutsi homes and other property in retaliation.

The International Commission of Jurists reported that all the elected Hutu members of both houses of parliament, and all the main Hutu leaders, 86 of them altogether, had been shot dead. Many other Hutus were also killed[1] by the Tutsi in an attempt to eliminate any Hutu threat to their hegemonic control of the country in which they were vastly outnumbered. For example, in the central province of Muramvya alone, more than 1,000 Hutu elites were killed by the Tutsi in 1965. And the violence and killings continued.

On 8 July 1966, Mwami Mwambutsa IV was deposed by his son who became Mwami (King) Ntare V in October the same year. The new king was 21 years old. He overthrew his father with the help of Michel Micombero who became the real ruler of the country, with Mwami

Ntare being only a figure head.

Mwami Ntare did not last long in "power" even as a mere figure head. He was overthrown less than two months later on 28 November 1966 by Micombero who proclaimed Burundi a republic and became the country's first president. He was 26. He also became brigadier general after promoting himself.

Remarkably, Micombero assumed power after a bloodless coup in a country known for bloodshed. Mwami Ntare had appointed Captain Micombero prime minister on 11 July 1966 because of the role he played in the July 8th coup in which King Mwambutsa IV was overthrown when he was supposedly in voluntary exile in Geneva, Switzerland.

A graduate of the Royal Military School in Brussels, Belgium, Micombero was the army chief of staff when he overthrew Mwami Mwambutsa.

But he later fell out with Mwami Ntare V and accused the new king of failing to discharge his responsibilities. He also accused the youthful, aristocratic ruler of allowing himself to be unduly influenced by his father, the deposed king.

After overthrowing Mwami Ntare V, Micombero formed the National Committee of the Revolution (CNR) entirely composed of army officers. Almost all of them were Tutsi. And the only political party allowed to operate in the country was also Tutsi: the Party of Unity and National Progress (UPRONA). The Hutu party, the Democratic Front of Burundi (FRODEBU), was banned. Captain Micombero was also promoted to colonel and given a seven-year term as president.

The most serious problem Micombero faced when he became president was the presence of tens of thousands of Tutsi refugees, and their king, Mwami Kigeri V, from Rwanda. They fled their homeland between 1959 and 1961 after a bloody conflict – starting with the Hutu mass uprising of November 1959 – in which the Hutu emerged victorious.

Many of the Rwandan Tutsis who had fled to Burundi were also armed. The presence of these Tutsis and their king, in a safe haven in Burundi, was viewed with apprehension by Hutu-dominated neighbouring Rwanda where they were determined to return and restore the Tutsi aristocracy.

Although before independence the Tutsi-dominated kingdoms of Ruanda and Urundi were administered jointly as Ruanda-Urundi by Belgium, they chose to separate after the Belgian colonial rulers relinquished control of their colonial territory.

Rwanda became a republic at independence, and Burundi remained a monarchy until 1966 when the Tutsi aristocracy was replaced by a republican form of government under Micombero.

When Burundi became a republic, her relations with Rwanda also improved. Both countries were now under the same political system. Both were republics. The monarchy in both countries was gone.

Micombero also tried to ease ethnic tensions in Burundi, but only half-heartedly. He imposed harsh rule on the country and silenced his critics within two years of seizing power. Most of those critics were Hutus who had been excluded from power. Therefore, instead of improving relations between the two ethnic groups, he alienated most Hutus. According to *Africa Contemporary Record 1968 – 1969*:

"Political expression in any way critical of the government had remained severely curbed in Burundi.

Six former ministers and parliamentarians were each sentenced to ten years imprisonment on December 26, 1968, for writing and distributing an open letter critical of the president.

Three others arrested in the case in May (1968) were imprisoned from three to seven years, and three were

70

acquitted.

Among those sentenced to ten years' imprisonment was the former president of the Legislative Assemby, Mr. Thadde Siryuyumisi."[2]

In 1969, President Micombero survived a coup attempt by some politicians and disgruntled elements in the army. Following the abortive coup, he consolidated his position by concentrating more power in his hands. And as head of the only legal political party in the country, the Unity and National Progress Party (UPRONA) which was Tutsi, he tolerated no opposition even from fellow Tutsis.

In 1970, Burundi adopted a new constitution. But it did little to liberalise his rule.

One of Africa's bloodiest conflicts erupted in April 1972 when Ntare V returned to Burundi from exile. President Micombero assured him in writing that nothing would happen to him if he returned home.

The deposed king returned to Burundi with dreadful results. An attempt by his supporters to reinstate him failed, and the rebellion was brutally suppressed by government troops. Ntare was "judged and immediately executed."[3]

Mwami Ntare's return coincided with the invasion of Burundi by Hutu exiles mostly based in Rwanda. The invasion was triggered by the brutal purge of Hutus from the military and the government, and by the vicious repression of Hutu peasants across the country by Tutsi soldiers.

There was no direct evidence, circumstantial or otherwise, showing that the Hutu living in Burundi joined the invasion. But given the intense hostility between the two ethnic groups, some probably did, and many undoubtedly supported the idea of dislodging the Tutsi from power by force. However, the invasion failed.

About 10,000 Tutsis were killed in the fighting. But it was the Hutu who suffered the most. The Tutsi-dominated government and army launched a brutal campaign of retaliation and terror against them which amounted to genocide. "The victorious Tutsis proceeded to massacre some 100,000 persons in six weeks, with possibly more slain by summer."[4]

More than 100,000 Hutus fled to Tanzania and Zaire (now Congo) in what had become an established pattern of forced migration in this highly unstable Great Lakes region which has undergone momentous upheavals through the years, with the two countries (Tanzania and Congo) acting as shock absorbers.

However, the refugees, from both Rwanda and Burundi, have never been fully welcome in Congo – in 1981, Zaire under Mobutu stripped the Banyamulenge Tutsis of their citizenship – because of ethnic hostilities and conflicts over land in the eastern part of the country. But they have found better reception in Tanzania. As Professor Harvey Glickman stated in "Tanzania: From Disillusionment to Guarded Optimism":

"Tanzania (has a track record of)...generous treatment of refugees and mediation of disputes that cause refugee flows....

After Zaire, Tanzania hosts the second-largest number of refugees in Africa. More than 700,000 – including a half million from Rwanda and about 200,000 from Burundi – are in camps in the northern and western parts of the country.

Burundians now comprise two generations of refugees. Thousands of Burundians crossed into Tanzania in 1963, fleeing the violence accompanying Burundi's first (abortive) coup. These earliest refugees were resettled and some achieved citizenship.

In 1980 tens of thousands of Rwandan refugees were offered citizenship.

A second wave of refugees from Rwanda entered in 1983, after expulsion from Uganda. Just under 100,000

Burundians have fled the latest surge of violence since 1993 (and sought refuge in Tanzania)."[5]

The ethnic violence will probably continue for years, as it has during the past several decades.

After the abortive April 1972 Hutu invasion of Burundi, the Hutu revolted again in May 1973 against the Tutsi. Another massacre of genocidal proportions followed. Tens of thousands of Hutus and thousands of Tutsis were killed. More refugees, mostly Hutu, fled to Tanzania and Zaire.

In 1976, the Minority Rights Group (MRG), a British organisation, accused Micombero's government of having systematically killed all Hutus who had more than secondary school education.[6]

On 1 November 1976, Lieutenant-Colonel Jean-Baptiste Bagaza overthrew Micombero in a military coup and became president. He was a distant cousin of Micombero. Both were members of the same clan.

A Tutsi himself and Belgian-educated political scientist, Bagaza promised to end civil strife, but with little prospect of success in such a deeply divided country.

In 1979, he was elected to lead the country's ruling party, UPRONA, in a rigged contest and which was almost exclusively Tutsi. The Hutu majority remained virtually disenfranchised.

In 1980, Bagaza established a "civilian government," making the Central Committee of Burundi's sole political party (UPRONA) the main legislative body to approve his decrees, and dissolved his military junta – the Supreme Revolutionary Council – composed of 30 army officers.

Meanwhile, as ethnic violence continued, former Burundian president, Michel Micombero, died of a heart attack in exile in Somalia on 16 July 1983. He was 43. According to *Africa Report*:

"Burundi's former president, Michel Micombero, died

73

of a heart attack on July 16 in Mogadishu, Somalia.

He came to power in 1966 after deposing King Ntare, and he ruled until his ouster in 1976 by Lieutenant-Colonel Jean Baptiste Bagaza, who sent Micombero into exile in Somalia.

Micombero began his career in the military, and then served as minister of defense, secretary of state, and prime minister before installing himself as president.

Once in office, Micombero attempted to reconcile the rift between the Hutu majority and the politically dominant Tutsi minority. He began by freeing Hutu political prisoners, but his rule quickly turned repressive. Following a 1972 attempted coup, his forces turned on the Hutu, killing 100,000 people.

In Somalia, President Mohammed Siad Barre declared a three-day period of mourning for Micombero."[7]

The Hutu-Tutsi conflict also involved the Roman Catholic church which incurred the wrath of the Tutsi-dominated government.

The Catholic clergy was suspected of sympathising with the Hutu majority, a charge which led to the expulsion of many foreign priests and other missionaries in 1985.

The vast majority of the people – Hutu and Tutsi – in both Rwanda and Burundi are Catholic, and the church has great influence in their lives, although it has not been able to resolve the ethnic conflict between the two groups. Ironically, Rwanda and Burundi are the two most Christian countries in Africa.

In May 1987, Major Pierre Buyoya overthrew Bagaza, his cousin. Buyoya was also Micombero's nephew.

The new military ruler introduced reforms intended to reduce ethnic tensions but whose implementation depended on the willingness of the Tutsi to do so.

Buyoya, who went on to rule Burundi for 13 years at different times (1987 – 1993 and 1996 – 2003), became the longest-ruling president in the country's history.

After he overthrew Bagaza, he formed a cabinet to reflect ethnic composition of the country. The majority of the cabinet members he appointed were Hutu. He also chose a Hutu prime minister and encouraged the Hutu to join the Tutsi-dominated army.

But these measures did little to weaken let alone end the Tutsi's hegemonic control of the country. Real power remained in the hands of the military junta which was dominated by Tutsis. The Hutu majority continued to suffer discrimination. They had only limited educational and economic opportunities and remained virtually disenfranchised in a country where they vastly outnumbered the Tutsi 6 to 1.

Burundi again descended into chaos in August 1988 when large-scale fighting between the Hutu and the Tutsi erupted, following an abortive coup attempt by the Hutu whose condition had hardly improved in spite of the reform measures introduced by Buyoya to liberalise the political process and achieve ethnic reconciliation:

"The Tutsi-run military government under Pierre Buyoya massacred an estimated 20,000 Hutus. U.N. Officials at refugee camps near the border with Rwanda told of soldiers chasing, machine-gunning, and bayoneting fleeing Hutus."[8]

Tens of thousands of Hutus fled to Tanzania. But most of them returned to Burundi by mid-1989. However, that was only temporarily, as a new wave of violence engulfed Burundi and the entire Great Lakes region during the 1990s.

On 2 June 1993, Melchior Ndadaye, a Hutu candidate of the Burundi Democratic Front (FRODEBU), won the presidency in the first democratic elections since independence in 1962. He defeated the incumbent military ruler, Pierre Buyoya, who was the candidate of the predominantly Tutsi party, UPRONA.

Ndadaye survived a coup attempt on July 3rd and was sworn in as president on July 10th.

Buyoya had allowed the elections to take place in fulfillment of his pledge to introduce democracy and allow the Hutu to participate fully in the political process. He also believed he was going to win the election because of his liberalisation programme – democratic reforms which had never been introduced before – which may have won him considerable support, so he believed, among the Hutu.

His commitment to egalitarianism, although lukewarm, earned him enemies among his fellow Tutsis, especially hardliners including his cousin Jean-Baptiste Bagaza whom he overthrew in 1987. They saw him as a traitor.

Ndadaye tried to improve relations between the Hutu and the Tutsi and appointed a female Tutsi, Sylvie Kinigi, as prime minister. He also appointed many Tutsis as members of his cabinet. And entire third of the cabinet members were Tutsi. He also granted amnesty to Jean-Baptiste Bagaza who was living in exile and freed political prisoners.

The president also tried to redress the ethnic imbalance across the spectrum and improve living conditions of the Hutu majority who had been deprived of opportunities by the dominant Tutsis through the years. He also introduced reforms in the army and the police to reduce control by the Tutsi. Many Hutus also got government posts originally held by the Tutsi after the landslide victory in the June 1993 election by the predominantly Hutu party, FRODEBU, further infuriating Tutsis.

The freedom of speech Ndadaye allowed also made things worse. Newspapers and the radio provided extensive coverage of the reforms introduced by Ndadaye but in a way that inflamed passions, especially among the Tutsi, who now felt they had been marginalised by the Hutu rulers, although the government was not dominated by Hutus. It was fairly representative of all the people of

Burundi and took into account concerns of the Tutsi in a country that was now under a Hutu president, a predominantly Hutu cabinet and parliament for the first time in the nation's history because of truly democratic elections Tutsis have always feared so much since they are vastly outnumbered by Hutus.

The changes Buyoya introduced and tried to implement angered many Tutsis who felt that their privileged position was being threatened by the new policies.

He did not last long in office. He was assassinated within four months, bayoneted to death by Tutsi soldiers on 21 October 1993 in a coup attempt engineered by Tutsi hardliners who wanted to restore Tutsi leadership of the country.

President Ndadaye's assassination infuriated the Hutu. But it also emboldened the Tutsi who saw their loss of power only as temporary.

The result was genocide in which more than 100,000 people, mostly Hutu, were massacred within one year after the assassination, and more than 500,000 fled to Tanzania, Rwanda, and Zaire.

Ndadaye's assassination was a turning point in the nation's history. It marked the beginning of the bloodiest and longest civil war in the history of Burundi. It lasted from 1993 until 2005. More than 300,000 people, mostly Hutu, died in the conflict. Some estimates put the death toll at 500,000.

The war formally ended when Pierre Nkurunziza, a Hutu and former rebel leader who fought the Tutsi, was sworn in as president in August 2005.

A few months after the civil war started in 1993, Cyprien Ntaryamira, another Hutu who had served as the minister of agriculture in the government of Ndadaye, was chosen by the parliament in January 1994 to be the president of Burundi. He was appointed to serve the remainder of Ndadaye's term which was almost the entire term since Ndadaye had been in office for only three months before he was assassinated.

Ntaryamira's appointment as president infuriated the Tutsi. And like his predecessor and fellow Hutu Melchior Ndadaye, he did not last long in office.

He died on 6 April 1994 together with the president of Rwanda, Juvénal Habyarimana, also a Hutu, after their plane was hit by a rocket over Kigali, Rwanda's capital, when they returned from Tanzania where they had participated in peace talks aimed at resolving the ethnic conflict between the Hutu and the Tutsi in both countries:

"The rockets were fired form the immediate vicinity of the Kigali airport, an area controlled by the Rwandan army."[9]

The shooting down of the plane was the beginning of a downward spiral for Rwanda. It was an incident which precipitated an orgy of killings in the Rwandan capital, Kigali, targeting Tutsis and Hutu moderates.

The killings spread rapidly, engulfing the whole country in what came to be one of the most horrific events in the history of mankind towards the end of the twentieth-century history.

The peace talks between the Hutu and the Tutsi which were held in the town of Arusha in northern Tanzania led to an agreement on the establishment of a coalition government in Rwanda. But it was bitterly opposed by Hutu extremists who did not want to share power with the Tutsi. And they are the ones who were suspected of having fired the rocket which hit the plane carrying the two Hutu presidents.

The Hutu blamed the Tutsi for shooting down the plane and, in retaliation for "killing" the two Hutu presidents, started massacring Tutsis.

The downing of the plane may have triggered the massacres, eventually leading to genocide, but the reasons for the genocide can not be explained in such simplistic terms.

And there would have been another major casualty on that plane, with wider implications for the entire region, had fate not intervened.

President Mobutu Sese Seko of Zaire who also attended the peace talks in Tanzania was supposed to have caught the same plane on his way back to Zaire but changed his mind at the last minute and delayed his departure, thus saving his life.

Although Hutu extremists were the prime suspects in the shooting of the plane, Tutsi hardliners were also suspected of having brought the plane down. Like their Hutu counterparts, they also had vehemently denounced the power-sharing agreement as a threat to their security and the very survival of their ethnic group.

It was never firmly established who fired the rocket which brought the plane down. Was it Hutu extremists? Or was it Tutsi hardliners?

What is clear is that circumstantial evidence indicated that it was probably Hutu soldiers who fired the rocket because its trajectory showed it was fired from an area controlled by the Hutu-dominated Rwandan army.

There were Hutu soldiers who were opposed to the concessions made by President Habyarimana at the peace talks in Tanzania and wanted him removed from office, by any means, in order to block implementation of the power-sharing agreement.

But others speculated that the people who killed President Habyarimana and his Burundian counterpart, Cyprien Ntaryamira, belonged to a different opposition group impatient with the delays in forming a coalition government of Hutus and Tutsis and blamed Habyarimana for that.

Whatever the case, the assassination of the two Hutu leaders provided Hutu extremists with an "excuse" to start killing Tutsis – whom they blamed for the murders – and Hutu moderates who wanted to share power with the Tutsi.

79

Within an hour of the announcement of the deaths of the two leaders, the killings began, raising suspicion that the massacres had been preplanned.

The tragic incident, shooting down of the plane, not only sparked massive carnage in Rwanda but led to an escalation of violence in Burundi where the Hutu were still enraged over the assassination of the country's first Hutu president, Ndadaye, who was brutally murdered by the Tutsi only a few months before. The assassination of another Hutu president of Burundi, Cyprien Ntaryamira – to the Hutu, by who else? – only stoked the flames.

Before the civil war broke out in Rwanda in April 1994 following the assassination of President Habyarimana, Burundi was in a much worse situation than Rwanda before October 1993 when its first Hutu president, Ndadaye, was assassinated. The country was plunged into chaos following the assassination, and everything was being done by the Tutsi-dominated government to placate and contain the Hutu, employing a combination of diplomacy and brutal suppression.

In September 1994, a power-sharing agreement was reached between the Tutsi-dominated party, the Union for National Progress (UPRONA) which constituted the official opposition, and the predominantly Hutu Democratic Front of Burundi (FRODEBU) which formed the democratically elected government left behind by the two assassinated Hutu presidents, Ndadaye and Ntaryamira.

But the coalition agreement was undermined by Tutsi extremists who denounced the moderate Tutsi prime minister, Anatole Kanyenkiko, as a sellout and finally forced him to leave the predominantly Hutu government.

The situation was further complicated by the fact that former FRODEBU interior minister, Leonard Nyangoma – frustrated by the inability of the Hutu-majority government to govern effectively because of constant undermining by the traditionally powerful Tutsi military and elite – had gone into exile and formed an opposition group.

His group was known as the National Council for the Defence of Democracy (CNDD). It had an armed wing, the Democratic Defence Front (FDD), which started waging guerrilla warfare in northern Burundi from its operational bases in South Kivu Province in eastern Zaire.

The fighting between Nyangoma's Hutu guerrillas and Burundi's Tutsi-dominated army escalated towards the end of 1995 and in early 1996, with the death toll among civilians, mostly Hutu, climbing rapidly. Most of them were killed by Tutsi soldiers in indiscriminate acts of "retaliation."

With the 1994 Rwandan massacre of almost one million Tutsis still fresh in their memories and indelibly etched in their collective psyche, the Tutsi in Burundi feared they would be victims of the same kind of holocaust at the hands of their "historical enemies," the Hutu.

Caught between escalating guerrilla warfare by the FDD Hutu rebels and brutal repression by the Tutsi-dominated army, President Sylvestre Ntibantunganya – another Hutu and FRODEBU's constitutionally eligible successor to his assassinated predecessor, Ntaryamira – was reduced to being no more than a ceremonial head of state, without functional utility, at the mercy of the Tutsi.

It was in the midst of all this that former President Pierre Buyoya, a Tutsi moderate, was returned to power following a Tutsi-led military coup on 25 July 1996 which ousted Ntibantunganya.

But Buyoya himself, although a Tutsi and a soldier and therefore a member of both the dominant ethnic group and the country's most powerful institution (the army), found himself in an untenable position. A moderate who allowed Burundi's first democratic elections to take place in June-July 1993 in which he lost to a Hutu (Ndadaye), he had many enemies among fellow Tutsis who saw him as a traitor for allowing such transfer of power to the Hutu majority. And when he was returned to power in the 1996 military coup, he could not stop the atrocities being committed by the Tutsi army against innocent Hutu civilians.

Hutu support for the rebels also kept on increasing, fuelled by the atrocities being perpetrated against them by Tutsi soldiers. And when Tanzania, Kenya and Uganda imposed economic sanctions on Burundi to punish Buyoya and his Tutsi colleagues for overthrowing the constitutionally chosen Hutu president, Ntibantunganya, who headed a democratically elected although powerless government of the FRODEBU party, the Hutu guerrillas of the Democratic Defence Front (DDF) capitalised on the economic embargo and intensified their military campaign against the Tutsi regime and Tutsi civilians.

The capital itself, Bujumbura, came under attack, raising fears of an imminent holocaust against the Tutsi reminiscent of the 1994 genocide in neighbouring Rwanda.

The economic sanctions imposed on Burundi were producing dividends, however limited, because of the impact they had on the army. But the embargo did not affect the FDD guerrillas who were operating out of eastern Zaire just across the border from Burundi. Even destruction of their bases in South Kivu Province by the Banyamulenge (with the help of Rwanda, Uganda and Burundi) towards the end of 1996 was not enough to neutralise them. Instead, they stepped up their offensive against Burundi's Tutsi regime.

Between July and October 1996, the guerrillas believed that their increased offensive was about to extract concessions from the military junta in Bujumbura whose intransigence led to escalation of the conflict. President Buyoya even started to talk about negotiating with the rebels; a very dangerous move which was strongly opposed by Tutsi hardliners including his cousin Jean-

Baptiste Bagaza whom he overthrew in 1987. It could very easily have cost him his life. Yet the economic sanctions seemed to be working, pushing the Tutsi regime towards the conference table. However, towards the end of October, things took an unexpected turn.

After the Hutu rebels were routed from Uvira in South Kivu Province, Zaire, by the Banyamulenge Tutsis on 26 October 1996, their leader Leonard Nyangoma fled to Tanzania where he met with Julius Nyerere, the former Tanzanian president and the force behind the diplomatic initiative to impose an economic embargo on Burundi who had been pushing for a negotiated settlement of the conflict.

But when Buyoya was asked to go to Nyerere's home in the village of Butiama in northern Tanzania for a meeting, he reneged on his promise, saying he had changed his mind and would not participate in any negotiations aimed at resolving the conflict. Tutsi hardliners gave him very little room to manoeuvre even if he had wanted to negotiate with the Hutu.

A few weeks after he refused to meet with Nyerere, he arrested former President Bagaza, his cousin, together with several other Tutsi extremist leaders; a move which gave him more freedom to operate and make his own decisions. However, with the peace process derailed, Nyangoma and his guerrillas stepped up their offensive against Buyoya's government and the Tutsi-dominated army.

The army failed to contain let alone neutralise the guerrillas and started rounding up Hutu civilians in northern Burundi and put them in concentration camps to "isolate" the insurgents; a policy which could partly be attributed to the failure of economic sanctions which had never, from the beginning, been intended to force Buyoya out of power but restore constitutional rule.

Economic Embargo

On 30 September 1996, African regional leaders agreed at a meeting in Arusha, Tanzania, to impose full economic sanctions on Burundi in response to the July 25 Tutsi-led military coup and appealed to the international community for support in enforcing the embargo.

They also demanded immediate talks between all parties within and outside Burundi. But they took no action on a report presented by military planners for armed intervention in the strife-torn country.

The secretary-general of the Organisation of of African Unity (OAU), Dr. Salim Ahmed Salim of Tanzania, confirmed the decision to impose economic sanctions on Burundi after the leaders held a summit meeting to discuss the military coup.

After more than five hours of talks, the leaders said in a statement: "The summit has decided to impose economic sanctions on Burundi and appeals to the international community to support these measures."[10] And as President Benjamin Mkapa of Tanzania put it: "This is a total economic blockade on Burundi. It was a unanimous decision. There was not a single dissenting voice."[11]

The leaders of Tanzania, Kenya, Uganda, Rwanda, Zaire, Ethiopia, Eritrea, Zambia, Cameroon, and OAU representatives led by the organisation's secretary-general, Salim Ahmed Salim, attended the summit. And the measures they agreed upon to punish Burundi's military regime were later formally ratified by the OAU and by the United Nations. Tanzania's President Mkapa who hosted the summit said a technical committee would spell out details when sanctions would start and how long they would last.

Burundi is one of the African countries which is highly vulnerable to such punitive sanctions. A small, desperately poor and landlocked nation, its economy was, even before the sanctions were imposed, already hard-hit by civil war and by the suspension of international aid because of its poor human rights record and the atrocities committed by the Tutsi army against the Hutu, especially since the brutal assassination of President Melchior Ndadaye. Because of its landlocked position, its neighbours could exercise enormous leverage on its government and help bring about fundamental change in the country by simply choking it off. It also relies almost entirely on Tanzania and Rwanda to export its coffee and tea, its main exports, and to import all its fuel and other goods.

But it is highly unlikely that Rwanda, a Tutsi-dominated state, would enforce full economic sanctions against fellow Tutsis in Burundi. And there is humanitarian concern involved in the implementation of punitive measures which hardly affect the economic wellbeing of those in power including their relatives and friends. For example, in 1996 alone, Burundi was in such a bad economic situation because of the civil war that the UN World Food Programme sent it 43,000 tons of food worth $28.5 million (USD) to alleviate the plight.

But sanctions can also be used to weaken and isolate an oppressive regime; encourage its opponents to escalate their campaign against it; turn its supporters against it because of the economic hardship and suffering caused by the sanctions; and force it to make meaningful concessions to its opponents and reach a negotiated settlement. It is in this context that the economic embargo imposed on Burundi must be viewed as an effective bargaining tool in conflict resolution in that embattled country.

The coup which prompted Burundi's neighbours to impose an economic embargo was a direct result of the Tutsi dissatisfaction with the coalition government under Hutu President Ntibantunganya; a dissatisfaction deeply rooted in the animosity and distrust between the two ethnic groups. This was clearly demonstrated by the fact that even power-sharing between them had failed to reduce – let alone end – the ethnic violence plaguing the country.

Many parts of Burundi were so wracked by violence that they were totally out of government control and had become virtually inaccessible. Only the most reckless would even think of going into those areas.

Then the power-sharing agreement, negotiated after the abortive Tutsi-led coup of October 1993 in which Hutu President Melchior Ndadaye was assassinated, collapsed because the Tutsi demanded more power.

On 24 July 1996, the Tutsi political party, UPRONA, withdrew from the coalition with FRODEBU, the Hutu party. The end of the coalition marked the end of the government.

The Tutsi prime minister, Antoine Nduwayo, was rendered powerless by fellow Tutsis; so was the Hutu president, Sylvestre Ntibantunganya, who fled to the American embassy in Bujumbura where he was given sanctuary.

The situation degenerated into chaos as marauding bands of club-wielding young Tutsis took over large sections of the capital Bujumbura with the tacit support of the Tutsi-dominated army which did nothing to stop them.

Then on the following day, 25 July, the army announced that it had seized power and that Major Perre Buyoya, the former military ruler, would be the leader of the new military regime.

The ouster of the coalition government did not come as a surprise. There had been rumours circulating in the capital and elsewhere that Tutsi hardliners in the army were about to execute a coup. The city was gripped with fear, and many people speculated that another genocide was imminent. According to a report from Bujumbura by *The Economist*, 27 July 1996:

"Seasoned visitors to Burundi's capital – which, cleansed of Hutus, now belongs to the 14 per cent

Burundians who are Tutsi – said they had never seen the city so fearful. Not, however, of a coup, let alone a fall of government. Burundians' overriding fear has been that extremists, on either side of the ethnic divide, could send the violence that has killed more than 150,000 people in the past three years spiralling into genocide.

Such fears seemed confirmed last weekend when 350 displaced Tutsis, mostly women and children, living in a settlement at Bugendena in central Burundi, were horribly slaughtered.

Reports by survivors suggest that their attack was masterminded by the rebel Hutu army led by Leonard Nyangoma from just across the border in Zaire, possibly in collusion with elements from the old Rwandan army, also in exile.

On July 23rd, when President Ntibantunganya tried to visit the scene of the massacre, he was stoned by Tutsi protesters and forced to beat a retreat – all the way to the American embassy."[12]

In fact, he was almost lynched and miraculously escaped from the mob.

The Hutu rebel attacks were met with a swift response from the Tutsi army which used them to justify its indiscriminate campaign of terror against Hutu civilians who were targeted mainly because of their ethnicity.

The army also targeted Rwandan Hutu refugees who settled in northern Burundi after they fled their country for fear of reprisals by the victorious predominantly Tutsi Rwandan Patriotic Front (RPF) for the 1994 genocide. And the fact that the refugee camps had some of the perpetrators of the genocide hiding among innocent civilian refugees made the campaign by Tutsi soldiers more credible when they targeted those camps.

However, the presence of Hutu extremists in the camps was also used by the Tutsi government to justify its mass expulsion of Rwandan Hutus from northern Burundi even when there was no need to do so:

"The forcible repatriation of several thousand Rwandan refugees from northern Burundi...began on July 19 (1996) just before the massacre (of 350 displaced Tutsis in a settlement at Bugendena in central Burundi towards the end of July).

Of the estimated 85,000 Rwandans (mostly Hutu) in Burundi, more than 13,000 have so far been crammed into lorries and dumped across the border."[13]

Many of them arrived in Rwanda only to find their homes, farms and property had been taken by Tutsi exiles who were among the one million Tutsis who returned to Rwanda after the genocidal Hutu regime collapsed in July 1994.

But in spite of what happened next door in Rwanda in 1994, a holocaust unprecedented in modern times in terms of magnitude and intensity in telescoped time (one million people slaughtered in 100 days at a rate five times faster than Hitler killed the Jews), the international community did nothing to avert a probable catastrophe in Burundi where low-intensity warfare was claiming countless lives, with a potential for another genocide may be even on a scale equal to or bigger than Rwanda's.

On 22 July 1996, the UN secretary-general, Boutros Boutros-Ghali, asked the Security Council to support a military intervention in Burundi under UN auspices. But his appeal fell on deaf ears.

In Africa itself, a regional East African intervention force – of Tanzanians, Ugandans, and Ethiopians – was being mobilised to cope with the situation. However, nothing went beyond the preparatory stage.

The crisis intervention force could not intervene without Burundi's approval. The Tutsi army itself, the most powerful institution in the country, was in no mood for that. And that was before the coup. Tutsi leaders became even more intransigent after that. Because of its enormous power, the army could veto any decision by the civilian government headed by the Hutu president, Ntibantunganya, and his Tutsi prime minister, Antoine Nduwayo.

The deteriorating security situation in the country had, in June 1996, prompted the civilian government to request military intervention from its East African neighbours before everything spun out of control. But the Tutsi vetoed it, with threats:

"Last month (in June 1996), Mr. Nduwayo was persuaded to join Mr. Ntibantunganya in 'inviting' such a force into Burundi to provide 'security assistance.'

'Traitor,' shouted his fellow-Tutsis. Under this attack, Mr. Nduwayo vacillated, eventually deciding that he resolutely opposed outside intervention, which, he said, would not only fail to prevent massacres but would make the situation worse."[14]

In opposing intervention, Nduwayo had partially rehabilitated himself with his fellow Tutsis many of whom agreed with him when he said the presence of foreign troops would only make things worse.

One main reason for this opposition is that throughout the history of the Hutu-Tutsi ethnic conflict in both Rwanda and Burundi, the Tutsi have repeatedly complained that neighbouring countries – Tanzania, Congo, Kenya, and Uganda (before Yoweri Museveni, of Tutsi ancestry himself, according to some reports, became Ugandan president) – favour the Hutu; a charge without foundation which former Tanzanian President Julius Nyerere dismissed as "nonsense," adding, "we have heard it before," when he was the chief mediator in Burundi's conflict and the main force behind the economic embargo imposed on the Tutsi regime in Bujumbura.

One of the most prominent and outspoken Tutsi leaders

who blamed Nyerere for favouring the Hutu was Charles Mukasi. There were also reports that Tutsi hardliners planned to assassinate Nyerere. A planned visit to Bujumbura by Nyerere during the mediation of the conflict was also cancelled for security reasons cited by the Tanzanian intelligence service.

The underlying argument by the Tutsi – who are Nilotic in origin but who are now also Bantu after centuries of intermarriage with the Hutu majority – is that the people of neighbouring countries take sides with the Hutu because the vast majority of them are Bantu (which is a linguistic designation, not a racial category, since there is no Bantu race) like the Hutu; totally ignoring the asymmetrical relationship between the two ethnic groups in both countries, with the Tutsi minority as the dominant group denying the Hutu majority equal rights and opportunity.

It is an observation that has been made even by foreign missionaries who, because of their sympathy towards the oppressed Hutu majority, were expelled from Burundi in 1985 by the Tutsi military regime led by Jean-Baptiste Bagaza. Many of them had worked there for years.

It was in an attempt to rectify this situation – of Hutu oppression by the Tutsi – that Burundi's neighbours imposed economic sanctions on the Tutsi-dominated state which deliberately functioned as an ethnocracy, for the Tutsi, more than anything else.

Some of the people who were vehemently opposed to the East African intervention force included many Tutsi hardliners in Burundi's army, several of whom were involved in the1993 abortive coup in which President Ndadaye was assassinated. They had an unfinished agenda which would be difficult to pursue in the presence of foreign troops.

Hutu rebels were also opposed to intervention. While their Tutsi enemies vetoed foreign intervention in order to maintain the status quo and preserve Tutsi supremacy, the

Hutu wanted the East African force kept out of Burundi so that they could pursue, without hindrance, their goal to end Tutsi hegemonic control of the country.

The crisis intervention force was supposed to protect government leaders including cabinet members and senior civil servants as well as vital institutions and installations such as banks, the post office, the airport and power plants. But security for the leaders and different establishments in the country would not have stopped the ethnic violence between the Tutsi army and the Hutu rebels. And it would not have saved the lives of innocent civilians, both Hutu and Tutsi, who were being slaughtered at will by the combatants, targeting them purely on ethnic basis.

The regional security force never, of course, intervened in Burundi. It was never invited by President Sylvestre Ntibantunganya and Prime Minister Antoine Nduwayo who had Tutsi hardliners breathing down their necks. And after their government was overthrown, that option was completely ruled out. It was now time to see whether or not economic sanctions would work, since it was obvious that the new Tutsi military regime had no intention of inviting the East African intervention force, let alone giving up power.

The sanctions began to have an impact soon after they were imposed. Within only a few days, many Burundians especially in the capital became fully aware of the stranglehold neighbouring countries, mainly Tanzania, had on their fragile economy.

Rwandan Tutsi rulers, out of solidarity with fellow Tutsis in Burundi, may have wanted to avoid enforcing the sanctions. But their ability to do so was severely limited because their country is landlocked and is itself dependent on Kenya for an outlet to the sea. Burundi, on the other hand, is heavily dependent on Tanzania for that. According to *The Wall Street Journal*, 5 August 1996:

"Gas stations shut down in Burundi's capital after Tanzania closed its border to impose an embargo to force out the new military-installed government. Meanwhile, a U.N. Report says Burundi's army massacred thousands of Hutus in April and May."[15]

The massacres had been going on – on a large scale – since October 1993 when President Ndadaye was bayoneted to death by Tutsi soldiers, plunging the country into chaos. And although the economic embargo did not stop the carnage, it caused a lot of hardship for the army. Fuel shortage restricted the army's mobility, and lack of goods and equipment in general, including spare parts, caused other logistical problems for the military because of the economic sanctions being enforced by Tanzania.

Of all the East African countries, Tanzania was in the best position to enforce the embargo even without the help of other countries because more than 70 per cent of Burundi's imports and exports got through her territory.

The Tanzanian government tightened the noose around Burundi to try to force the Tutsi military junta to relinquish power by blocking oil and tanker trucks and lorries and other vehicles at the border. As a senior Tanzanian official said on 5 August 1996: "The border is closed. Nothing is going in and nothing is going out."[16]

But, in spite of the sanctions, the Tutsi were determined to hang on to power at any cost because of what they believe, rightly or wrongly, to be a threat to their very existence and survival as a people.

Vastly outnumbered by the Hutu, they fear they will perish unless they are the sole rulers of both Rwanda and Burundi; an uncompromising stand – despite professions to the contrary by the Tutsi – which has made power sharing impossible. Any concessions they have made to the Hutu have been minimal and have not loosened their grip on power, thus perpetuating the ethnic conflict.

Therefore any meaningful change has to be pursued

through a combination of punitive measures and diplomacy with the help of the neighbouring countries and the rest of the international community as happened in the case of apartheid South Africa. And that is not a far-fetched analogy.

Tutsi domination and oppression of the Hutu is another form of apartheid; it is black apartheid. But security concerns of the Tutsi as a vulnerable minority if they were to lose power or play a subordinate role in both Rwanda and Burundi where they are vastly outnumbered by the Hutu must also be taken into account.

Tanzania was the first country to enforce the embargo against Burundi, not only to oust the Tutsi military regime but also to help the Hutu actively participate in the political process in a meaningful way. Although the African leaders who imposed the sanctions did not explicitly state that their intention was to remove the Tutsi minority regime from power and replace it with a democratic government, that is exactly what they intended to do when they approved the embargo.

Even Rwanda, a Tutsi state, supported the sanctions, although only symbolically by signing the embargo agreement. In what amounted to no more than a symbolic gesture, Rwanda's foreign affairs minister announced on 5 August 1996 that his country would soon join the sanctions effort. Yet no one took him seriously.

Ethnic solidarity among the Tutsi is paramount and transcends regional interests. The powerful Tutsi minority in Rwanda sympathise with their kinsmen in Burundi and will not do anything to make them suffer regardless of what other regional leaders say.

The immediate effect of the sanctions was petroleum shortage. But the embargo had an impact in other areas as well. Commodities traders said the embargo had doubled the price of salt and other items and pushed up the price of other goods, some of which were no longer available on the market.

Around the same time, South Africa's Deputy President Thabo Mbeki arrived in Tanzania for talks with President Benjamin Mkapa on the Burundi crisis. South African President Nelson Mandela, who had been under increasing pressure to become directly involved in action against Burundi, said his country would act as a part of regional and continental efforts to bring about fundamental change in the landlocked East African country.

On 4 August 1996, Burundi's military ruler Major Pierre Buyoya denied again that he had executed a coup. He went on to say that his action was "an operation to save a people in distress. After all, it is better to face sanctions than to be killed. Countries which have not yet understood the change, particularly Tanzania, will understand."[17]

Buyoya's sentiments on the economic embargo were echoed by the United Nations. On 7 August, the UN made a passionate appeal to Tanzania and Kenya for permission to send food aid to more than 700,000 war refugees in Burundi.

The two countries imposed a tight air, road and water embargo on the landlocked nation which had a major impact because of their access to the sea. Both are bordered by the Indian Ocean. And a sustained embargo – especially by these two countries – could, at the very least, have brought down the Tutsi military junta and paved the way for a return to constitutional order.

As the embargo continued, blockading the coffee- and tea-producing nation to try to force the military regime to restore civilian rule, Major Buyoya said in an interview published on August 7th that he was willing to negotiate with the Hutu if they laid down their weapons. He told the French daily Le Figaro: "There will be a national debate. We'll find a solution."

He also pledged to put an end to "abuses and mistakes" after UN observers reported that thousands of Hutu civilians had been killed in recent months: "In a civil war, abuses and mistakes are possible," he said. "We will do all

94

we can to put an end to this. We will use discipline to fight against it."[18]

Buyoya also pledged "all guarantees" for the security of former President Ntibantunganya whom he overthrew and who took refuge in the American embassy in Bujumbura. He said about the ousted president: "I have also suggested he participate in the institutions working for the transition."[19]

UN officials said unless Tanzania and Kenya allowed humanitarian aid to pass to Burundi, the plight of those in need would dramatically deteriorate. In a letter to President Benjamin Mkapa of Tanzania and President Daniel arap Moi of Kenya, the United Nations promised to "put into place a framework that will ensure food reaches only those it is intended for."[20]

Uganda joined the blockade on August 7th, and the state-owned Air Burundi had only one foreign destination, Kigali, the capital of neighbouring Rwanda, another Tutsi-dominated state, which said it would not enforce the sanctions.

Rwanda's vice president and defence minister, General Paul Kagame, the country's most powerful man and *de facto* ruler, told BBC in an interview: "We are going to work with them and help them find a solution."[21].

He was critical of the seven-nation African summit which imposed the economic embargo, saying a mechanism should have been put in place so that the imposition of the sanctions was not done on a country-by-country basis.

But the main and probably only reason why Kagame refused to enforce the embargo was his government's sympathy for fellow Tutsis in Burundi; the kind of ethnic solidarity and ethnocentrism that has helped ignite and fuel tribal warfare in this highly combustible region through the years.

Had he cared about justice, he would have frankly acknowledged Tutsi oppression of the Hutu as the main problem in both Rwanda and Burundi, at the very least as one of the major problems, just as was the case in Rwanda where the Hutu ruled from 1962 to 1994 and discriminated against the Tutsi under a brutal Hutu ethnocracy which also instigated the 1994 holocaust in which almost one million Tutsis perished.

As Buyoya vacillated, without fully committing himself to negotiations with the Hutu for ethnic and pragmatic considerations (Tutsi hardliners could kill him if he made major or too many concessions to the Hutu, and his people, the Tutsi, would be out of power if he re-introduced democracy as he did in 1993), the East African leaders calibrated a graduated response to his initiatives – or lack thereof – to induce him to make fundamental changes short of calling for his ouster.

Not asking him to step down was itself a diplomatic tactic. It was intended to encourage him to cooperate and work with Tutsi moderates to keep Tutsi hardliners at bay; most of the hardliners would like to overthrow him and derail the peace process. However, regional leaders were emphatic in their demand. According to *The Economist*, 3 August 1996:

"They all called for an immediate return to constitutional order in Burundi, with the restoration of parliament and the unbanning of (political) parties.

They stopped short of demanding the reinstatement of ex-President Sylvestre Ntibantunganya...And they also postponed their call for foreign intervention, giving Mr. Buyoya until mid-August to implement the reforms."[22]

Although the regional leaders postponed their call for a crisis intervention force to intervene in Burundi, they still appealed to the international community to support them in enforcing the economic embargo. Buyoya reciprocated by appointing a Hutu prime minister, not only as a gesture of goodwill to the East African leaders who imposed the sanctions, but also as an effort to ease ethnic tensions and initiate meaningful dialogue with the Hutu.

It is a fact of life in relations among nations that countries have temporary friends but permanent interests. That explains why Rwanda and Uganda, both friends of Burundi, joined the call to isolate the Tutsi regime in Bujumbura, although Rwanda's protest was only symbolic.

But it is clear why the other neighbouring countries imposed the economic embargo on Burundi, besides their desire to see a restoration of constitutional order in that embattled nation.

The holocaust in Rwanda which sent waves of refugees pouring across their borders was still fresh in their minds. They could contemplate a scenario similar to that, unfolding in Burundi, if they did not arrest the situation. Otherwise they would have to prepare for the worst: be inundated with an influx of refugees, should Burundi collapse and descend into anarchy.

Therefore it was also purely a matter of national interest why Tanzania and other countries wanted to restore civilian rule in Burundi before millions of refugees started flooding them.

But prospects for a negotiated settlement of the ethnic conflict remained bleak, even as the embargo was being applied to achieve this goal.

The gulf between the two sides had widened even further when the Tutsi army cleansed Bujumbura virtually of all Hutus in 1995. The capital was now inhabited almost exclusively by the Tutsi; hardly a sign of good intentions towards the Hutu majority who have always been excluded from power and denied equal opportunity in all areas.

. Even the appointment of Pascal Firmin Ndimira, a Hutu – who had been agriculture minister in 1994, and vice-chancellor of Bujumbura University – as prime minister, did nothing to bring the two sides any closer. "Mr. Buyoya has said he will talk to Leonard Nyangoma's

Hutu rebels who operate from Zaire, controlling large tracts of land in northern Burundi, but only if they first lay down their arms. For his part, Mr. Nyangoma has vowed to go on mobilising the Hutu people until Mr. Buyoya and his Tutsi entourage capitulate."[23]

The Hutu majority had few illusions about Buyoya, despite his professions of good intentions. He was strongly suspected of having instigated the 1993 coup attempt which led to President Melchior Ndadaye's death and that of up to 100,000 other Burundians, mostly Hutu. The suspicion had credibility because it was backed up by UN investigators in Burundi.

And former President Jean-Baptiste Bagaza, who was overthrown by Buyoya in 1987, added fuel to the UN report when he implicated his rival (who was also his cousin) in the October 1993 abortive coup which took place only about four months after Buyoya lost the election to Ndadaye.

But many Tutsis, probably the majority, remained unperturbed by Buyoya's alleged complicity in Ndadaye's assassination, thus adding credibility to the charge that he was indeed involved in the murder in order to neutralise Hutu attempts to gain political power and perpetuate Tutsi hegemonic control of the country. And the Tutsi remained defiant even in the face of a sustained economic embargo. By mid-August 1996, most foreigners left Burundi as the sanctions continued to inflict pain on this landlocked, impoverished nation.[24]

Yet the choices have always been clear in this perennial conflict. The ethnic violence will continue for as long as the Hutu majority are excluded from power; and for as long as the Tutsi minority continue to fear that they will be exterminated.

Economic sanctions could not solve this dilemma and even failed to dislodge the Tutsi from power. But that is mainly because they were not fully enforced on sustained basis even if they had to go on for years to achieve the goal: to choke off the Tutsi-dominated state and enable the Hutu majority achieve equality with the Tutsi minority in a country that equally belongs to them. Therefore, in one way, Tutsi solidarity prevailed.[25]

And there is no doubt that ethnic nationalism will continue to play a central role in the volatile politics of the region for many years and can be contained only when the Tutsi-dominated states of Rwanda and Burundi truly become pluralistic societies with extensive devolution of power probably in a confederation of ethnostates.

The ethnic problems in these two countries require radical and innovative solutions, including separation, which may or may not be applicable or necessary in other African contexts.

Rationale for Intervention

African countries have been pathetically inept at settling their own conflicts through the years since independence in the sixties. They have, instead, relied on foreign intervention to save them – from themselves.

But the involvement of the East and Central African states in Burundi's crisis gave some hope that Africans have the capacity and the determination to solve their own problems without begging foreigners to do that for them, thus making a mockery of their independence.

The intervention by Burundi's neighbours, although limited, was endorsed by the Organisation of African Unity (OAU) – whose solid reputation in conflict resolution rests on its unenviable status as a prestigious debating club and, as Nyerere put it, "a trade union of tyrants" in a move which was a dramatic departure from its avowed policy of non-intervention in the internal affairs of member states.

Tanzania, Kenya, Uganda, Ethiopia, Zaire, and Zambia, minus Rwanda, severed commercial, air and road links to Burundi; not only to exert pressure on its fragile economy in order to force the Tutsi military regime to capitulate, but also to send a warning to potential coup makers and aspiring military dictators that coups will no longer be tolerated in the region and elsewhere on the continent; and that Africans don't need external intervention to settle their disputes.

Usually, Buyoya's seizure of power in July 1996 would have been virtually ignored or simply accepted by other African states as just another change of government and a ritual of African politics – which was none of their business as long as it took place outside their borders.

Since the founding of the OAU in Addis Ababa, Ethiopia, in May 1963, member states have upheld the principle of non-intervention with religious devotion, and colonial boundaries inherited at independence as sacrosanct. Thus, when Nigeria was plunged into a civil war (1967 – 1970) which could have led to the annihilation of an entire people – the Igbos of Eastern Nigeria who seceded from the federation and declared independence as the Republic of Biafra, had they not surrendered – most African countries, hence, officially, the OAU, refused to exert enough pressure and diplomatic influence on the Nigerian federal military government to induce it to stop the war it was waging against its own people and seek a negotiated settlement. This approach was flatly rejected at the OAU summit of the African heads of state in Algiers, Algeria, in September 1968. According to *Africa Research Bulletin*:

"At a plenary meeting, Tanzania, Zambia, Gabon and the Ivory Coast (the only African countries which recognised Biafra as an independent state) urged that the OAU should demand an immediate ceasefire in the Nigeria war followed by renewed negotiations between the two sides. This view was opposed by many speakers who supported the majority view that the war was an internal

100

Nigerian affair and that Nigerian territorial integrity must be maintained at all costs."[26]

If the massacre of the Igbo in Northern Nigeria and the potential for their extermination during the civil war was Nigeria's internal affair and was a price worth paying to save the Nigerian federation, then the persecution of black people in South Africa under apartheid was equally South Africa's internal affair. Yet other African countries went up in arms, as they vigorously protested and supported the freedom fighters against the apartheid regime.

President Julius Nyerere once addressed this subject with regard to non-intervention in the internal affairs of other countries. He said when an entire people are targeted for discrimination and even extermination, it ceases to be a an internal affair and becomes a matter of concern for all mankind.

That was clearly the case with the Igbos in Nigeria where tens of thousands were massacred and up to 2 million of them perished in the war; it was also the case with South Africa where the apartheid regime espoused the doctrine of white supremacy, oppressing blacks and other non-whites.

And that is clearly the case with Rwanda and Burundi where both the Hutu and the Tutsi have been victims of genocide, only in varying degrees, through the years, killing each other. The crisis calls for intervention whether the rulers, Hutu or Tutsi, like it or not.

But that is not the logic of African leaders. They contend otherwise.

The massacre of about 500,000 – some estimates say 800,000 – people in Uganda under Idi Amin (at least 150 people were killed every day); President Masie Nguema's 11-year reign of terror during which one-third of the population of Equatorial Guinea – about 100,000 people – fled into exile and an estimated 40,000 were tortured and killed; and the 1994 Rwandan genocide were all matters of internal affairs in which other African countries had no business interfering, as indeed was the case. None interfered in those countries, except Uganda when Tanzania got rid of Amin.

In all those cases, other African countries said nothing, and did nothing, to protest or try to stop the pogroms.

By the same criterion, the brutal suppression of the Hutu by the Tutsi army and security forces in Burundi – and in Rwanda by the predominantly Tutsi Rwandan Patriotic Front (RPF) since it seized power in 1994 – is an internal affair to be handled by the Tutsi themselves.

Yet in a complete reversal, the OAU said, "No," in the case of Burundi and supported the initiative by its neighbours to impose economic sanctions on the Tutsi regime to try to force it out of office.

Besides its desire to solve its own problems, Africa is also aware that the rest of the world does not care much about the continent, if at all, except when the interests of the world powers are at stake.

But there are also several reasons for that – why the rest of the world doesn't care about Africa. There is compassion deficit. There is also fatigue, with other people, non-Africans, asking: When are African wars and other major problems – corruption, tyranny, tribalism, poor governance, economic mismanagement, lack of transparency, outright theft by leaders who raid national coffers with impunity, to name only a few – when are all these problems going to end?

There are also considerations of national interest: What do the big powers and other countries have to gain or lose by intervening in or by staying out of African conflicts?

Then there is racism: The victims of ethnic cleansing in Kosovo "look just like us and like our children," unlike those in Rwanda and Burundi. "We even give ice cream to the children in Kosovo. They're happy and even play soccer outside because they are well taken care of, by us," yet "we have no money, we can't afford food for starving

African refugees, not even cheap maize flour to make porridge which is a whole meal for them – and which is all they need. They aren't used to anything good like our people in Kosovo."

So Africans have to learn to be on their own – we have to learn to depend on ourselves.

After the debacles of Somalia, Liberia, and Angola, and an almost total lack of interest in the plight of Sierra Leone despite ardent pleas to the international community for help, Africans know that the United Nations will not rush to rescue them.

Sometimes there are legitimate reasons for that.

UN peace keepers were killed and run out of Somalia; they were "exhausted" in Liberia; expelled from Angola; refused to intervene in Rwanda where they could have saved the Tutsi and prevented the genocide; stayed out of Sierra Leone until late in 1999 and, even then, they were mostly Nigerians who were already there constituting the bulk of the West African peacekeeping force and simply changed hats from ECOMOG to UN; and also did not intervene in Burundi and other hot spots across the continent.

After months of delay and lukewarm efforts to find a diplomatic solution to the conflict in Burundi, the UN refused to intervene as the country degenerated into chaos. The Security Council ruled out military intervention but offered no alternative or other options to resolve the conflict; yet another reminder to Africans that you are on your own.

Such UN indifference and OAU's unwillingness or incapacity to act allowed Julius Nyerere, the former president of Tanzania, to take the initiative in trying to resolve the conflict in Burundi; a role which enabled him to exert great influence during the crisis.

For months before the July 1996 coup, he led mediation efforts which brought the two sides together but without resolving the conflict because of the intransigence of both parties, especially the Tutsi who were determined to perpetuate themselves in power. In response to that, he promised "peace enforcement" if the rival parties refused to negotiate and make meaningful concessions. It is this 'peace enforcement" which led to the imposition of economic sanctions on Burundi.

As the sanctions began to bite, Burundi's response was swift, invoking moral arguments as well, to try to undermine the legitimacy and credibility of the embargo as a tool of conflict resolution. But that did not dissuade Tanzania, Burundi's neighbour and direct access to the sea – and probably the most strategically located country in the alliance of embargo supporters, with Kenya being next because of her access to the Indian Ocean like Tanzania but not Burundi's immediate neighbour – from enforcing the economic sanctions.

The other countries also enforced the sanctions in varying degrees, with Uganda doing so only half-heartedly because of her friendship with Burundi, while Rwanda did nothing – besides her symbolic gesture of endorsing the embargo. Without Tanzania's participation, the economic sanctions would have had very little impact on Burundi.

By 10 August 1996, more than 2,000 metric tons of UN food destined for refugee camps in Burundi were being held up in Dar es Salaam, Tanzania, in compliance with the embargo.

The Tanzanian *Sunday News* (the sister paper of the *Daily News*), 11 August 1996, quoted officials in Kigoma, the Tanzanian port on Lake Tanganyika through which most of the Burundi-bound traffic passes, as saying three ships loaded with food had been stopped from sailing to Burundi's capital Bujumbura.[27]

The impact of the sanctions was officially acknowledged by the Burundian government.

Burundi's new foreign affairs minister, Luc Rukingama, said on August 10th in Brussels, Belgium, that the embargo was having a disastrous impact on his

104

country's economy and hurting the most vulnerable people:

"Now it's a matter of explaining, of informing and showing that this embargo is politically without foundation, completely unproductive, morally unacceptable and a catastrophe economically. (Sanctions) work against the children, women, old people and all the men of the country."[28]

Rukingama became minister of foreign affairs in a transitional government formed on 2 August 1996, about one week after President Sylvestre Ntibantunganya was overthrown.

The Tutsi military rulers claimed they seized power to prevent genocide in Burundi. Yet it was their attempt to seize power in October 1993 which triggered the genocide of more than 200,000 (some say 500,000) people, mostly Hutu, within three years after the newly elected President Melchior Ndadaye was bayoneted to death by Tutsi soldiers; an assassination that enraged his kinsmen, the Hutu, who started killing Tutsis, thus provoking an extremely brutal retaliatory response from the Tutsi army which went on the rampage, massacring hundreds of thousands of Hutu civilians including children. No-one was spared. Every Hutu was prime target.

Therefore, there was no reason to believe why a complete takeover by the Tutsi army would stop the very genocide it had started and which it actually had no intention of stopping, as was clearly demonstrated by the extremely brutal repression and continued indiscriminate mass killings of Hutu civilians by Tutsi soldiers even after Buyoya seized power in July 1996.

Since the coup, both sides continued to accuse each other of committing atrocities. And the victims were not getting enough attention, if any, with sanctions compounding the problem.

The international medical charity, Doctors Without Borders, said in August 1996 that the economic embargo was blocking medicine from reaching the victims, and supplies in Burundi were drying up.[29] But in spite of all that, the regional leaders tightened the sanctions.

On August 16th, regional foreign ministers meeting in Kampala, Uganda, banned travel to their countries by the members of Burundi's military regime. Zambia also joined the blockade.

However, the ministers decided to allow medical supplies and food for Rwandan Hutu refugees in Burundi to pass across the border. They also set up a committee, based in Kenya, to coordinate the embargo.[30]

In a coordinated strategy – augmented by the impact of the embargo – to undermine the legitimacy of the Tutsi military regime, Burundi's ousted Hutu president, Sylvestre Ntibantunganya, insisted that he still was the legal head of state, in spite of the fact that he was overthrown and was now a refugee in the American embassy where he was admitted on July 23rd, two days before the coup.

In a statement from him issued by his predominantly Hutu Front for the Democratisation of Burundi (FRODEBU) on August 19th, Ntibantunganya said that Burundi's only legal institutions were his presidency, the National Assembly, and his government.[31]

The statement was released in Nairobi, Kenya, where his party had offices, waging a campaign against the Tutsi military junta. It was a direct response to what Buyoya did after he seized power: he claimed the presidency, formed a government, suspended the National Assembly, and banned all political parties. As Ntibantuganya stated: "The Parliament elected on June 3, 1993, remains the sole legitimate legislative institution."[32]

He thanked neighbouring states for their coordinated effort to punish the Tutsi military regime and force Buyoya to relinquish power.

Their involvement in Burundi's crisis set a precedent in the regional context. No such coordinated effort had been made before to deal with a regional crisis. That is why Idi Amin's reign of terror went unanswered and lasted for more than 8 years (25 January 1971 – 10 April 1979 when the capital Kampala fell), as most of the neighbours looked the other way. And that is why nothing was done by the East African countries to stop the 1994 genocide in Rwanda.

But in spite of such retrogressive isolationism, their 1996 intervention in Burundi had been preceded by another intervention in the region, although on unilateral basis. And that was by Tanzania when Idi Amin annexed 710 square miles of her territory in November 1978, triggering a six-month full-scale war which led to his downfall. He fled on 11 April 1979 in a helicopter and went into exile in Libya.

Economic sanctions against Burundi could have achieved the same objective – ouster of a reprehensible regime – had the two countries in the embargo effort, Tanzania and Kenya, used their strategic location as coastal states to compel the rest to enforce the punitive measures.

Kenya could – and should – have denied both Uganda and Rwanda access to the sea, totally blocking their exports and imports, unless they isolated Burundi entirely. And both Kenya and Tanzania should have blocked Burundi's imports and exports until the Tutsi regime relinquished control and allowed the Hutu majority to share power with the Tutsi minority on the basis of a mutually acceptable formula. Tanzania by herself could have enforced a total blockade of Burundi's exports and imports passing through her territory.

That is probably the only way the Tutsi regime in Burundi could have been forced to capitulate, short of military intervention – an unrealistic scenario in the absence of a regional crisis intervention force.

The survival of the Tutsi military regime in Burundi was one more sad chapter in the history of the country and of this highly volatile region. The military rulers only succeeded in perpetuating what is probably the most violent ethnic conflict – Hutu versus Tutsi – on the entire continent.

Its resolution requires bold initiatives and compromises unprecedented in the history of post-colonial Africa.

Part Three:

Perennial Conflict: The Road to Nowhere

AT THE CENTRE of the Great Lakes crisis is the fate of the powerless Hutu majority whose disenfranchisement guarantees only one thing: perpetual conflict in both Rwanda and Burundi, with its repercussions spreading throughout the region.

Although the Tutsi minority are in power, they are still not secure precisely because they continue to deny the Hutu majority the security they themselves don't have, but which they could have if they conceded the legitimacy of the Hutu demand for equality – one simple word, "equality," whose meaning Tutsi leaders pretend they don't understand or are incapable of comprehending.

The Hutu's subordinate status as a disenfranchised and

powerless majority has been clearly demonstrated by the brutal mistreatment they have endured under Tutsi domination through the years, including their predicament as permanent refugees being shuttled back and forth across borders as if they have no country. They belong somewhere, yet they belong nowhere.

The situation in Burundi about a month after the July 1996 military coup is illustrative of their predicament as a "homeless" people. According to a report from Butare, Rwanda, in the *International Herald Tribune*:

"Hundreds of Rwandan Hutu refugees fled Burundi on Tuesday (20 August) for their equally troubled homeland despite assurances from Burundi's new Tutsi leader, Major Pierre Buyoya, that he was opposed to any expulsions.

UN officials said 500 Rwandans had arrived by noon Tuesday at Musenge transit camp outside Butare. A convoy of trucks packed with a total of 1,200 more refugees was also heading from Magara camp on its way to Butare.

The refugees accuse the Tutsi-dominated Burundian Army of harassment and say they fear for their lives.

About 2 million Rwandan Hutu fled their homeland to Zaire, Tanzania and Burundi in 1994 after Tutsi rebels defeated the Hutu-led army and ousted the government, blamed for the genocide of up to a million Tutsi and moderate Hutu.

Major Buyoya pledged Tuesday to protect the refugees after they complained of harassment and beatings from his army....

Shortly after the July 25 coup that brought him to power, Major Buyoya ordered an end to expulsions of Rwandan Hutu refugees."[1]

But the expulsions continued, and the Hutu ended up in their homeland where they found themselves not welcome by the Tutsi who blamed them for the 1994genocide, despite the fact that not every Hutu supported or took part in the massacres.

This is just one case which demonstrates the deep hatred and mistrust between the two groups, and for perfectly understandable reasons in spite of the injustice the Hutu majority have suffered through the years, as did the Tutsi under a brutal Hutu regime in Rwanda – for 32 years from July 1962 to July 1994 – which consolidated a Hutu ethnocracy.

It is a dilemma both groups, in both countries (Rwanda and Burundi), will continue to face for years: how to reconcile legitimate fear of the Tutsi, that they could be exterminated if they relinquish power, with the Hutu's genuine aspirations for equality and power as a legitimate democratic majority. They may not be divided by an implacable wall of hostility, but the perception exists even among themselves that they are, considering the asymmetrical relationship that exists between the two groups in both countries, with the Tutsi perpetuating their dominance.

Under such circumstances, even partition of the two countries along ethnic lines into independent Hutu and Tutsi ethnostates becomes an attractive proposition in order to achieve peaceful coexistence, reprehensible as this option is, especially in the context of Pan-Africanism. But if that is the only way the two countries can end the bloodshed, so be it. Even some African leaders, such as Kenyan President Daniel arap Moi, have endorsed this as a viable solution; Moi said so publicly in 1996. Other leaders have done so quietly.

What is even more repugnant is the willingness of many African leaders to sanction ethnocide – as happened against the Igbos in Nigeria during the civil war, and in Rwanda and Burundi against both the Hutu and the Tutsi – regardless of the cost, just for the sake of African unity: keep African countries united, don't let them break up into smaller, weaker nations, even if we have to loose millions

111

of lives in the name of African unity or just to maintain the territorial integrity of our countries.

That is what has prevented them from recognising Somaliland as an independent state in spite of the fact that it has all the attributes of a sovereign entity as a functional state contrasted with the rest of Somalia which is a wasteland.

In the case of Rwanda and Burundi, it is the Hutu who – despite their weakness as a powerless people – have the capacity to take bold initiatives towards conflict resolution in an ethnic context because of their unassailable status as the vast majority of the population in both countries. And that entails self-determination in the areas they dominate, especially for northwestern Rwanda which could become a microstate and the nucleus of a larger independent Hutu ethnostate, providing impetus and legitimacy to the dynamics of secession in both Rwanda and Burundi.

Both Rwanda and Burundi also can be divided into autonomous regions on ethnic basis, reducing the power of the central government which has caused so much misery for so many people when it is in the hands of one ethnic group or the other.

It will be very difficult to achieve either goal in the context of Rwanda and Burundi because the Hutu and the Tutsi are so integrated in their lives, inextricably linked by geography – living in the same villages; by history and family ties through the centuries, so much so that there are really no "pure" Hutus or "pure" Tutsis, if there ever were.

Yet, for practical purposes, the two groups do exist, tragically demonstrated by bloody conflicts between them on ethnic basis through the years.

But if the people themselves want to do it, they can do it: form independent ethnostates, or create autonomous regions on ethnic basis while maintaining the territorial integrity of both countries.

Outright declaration of independence for northwestern

Rwanda, even for southeastern Burundi, or any other Hutu stronghold may be the only way to initiate a vigorous national debate on the status of the two countries as viable political entities or as prime candidates for dissolution on the basis of a mutually acceptable formula which does not rule out the establishment of independent ethnostates or even a confederation of those states.

The Hutu and the Tutsi are no more compatible than the Jews and the Arabs are in Palestine; nor are the Greeks and the Turks in Cyprus, already partitioned by Turkey, despite the refusal by the international community to recognise the Turkish area on the island as a legal sovereign entity.

In the case of the Jews and the Arabs, the national question can be resolved in the context of a dynamic compromise conceding the legitimacy of an independent Palestinian state as the final solution.

The alternative is perpetual conflict, as is the case in Rwanda and Burundi where Tutsi armies and security forces have wreaked havoc through the years, targeting Hutus, for both legitimate and illegitimate reasons: fighting the rebels, and killing innocent civilians for no reason other than that they are Hutu – and therefore rebel "supporters" or "rebels" themselves.

In Burundi, the scale of human devastation was amply demonstrated soon after the July 1996 military coup, belying the claim by the military head of state, Major Pierre Buyoya, and his Tutsi compatriots that the coup was carried out to stop genocide and end the civil war.

The coup made things worse, while the Tutsi cheered. They were glad a Hutu president had been removed from office after being assassinated, and they were now back in power, although they really never lost it, since they were – and have always been – in control of the army which is the most powerful institution in the country.

The Hutu were furious. They saw the coup, and justifiably so, as an usurpation of power from duly constituted authority, a Hutu president, who had the constitutional mandate to rule.

This clash of perceptions and interests inevitably led to increased bloodshed as tensions escalated.

The Hutu were further enraged when they learned that top military officers – Tutsis including Pierre Buyoya himself – instigated and masterminded the assassination of President Melchior Ndadaye.

The revelation was made during the very same time when Tutsi atrocities before, during, and after the coup were also getting ample media coverage. According to the *International Herald Tribune*:

"The human rights group Amnesty International said Thursday (August 22, 1996) that more than 6,000 people were reported to have been killed in Burundi in the three weeks following the army coup on July 25.

Amnesty, which is based in London, said the human rights situation in Burundi continued to deteriorate despite promises by the new Tutsi military ruler, Pierre Buyoya, to end ethnic killings.

It said it had learned that at least 4,050 unarmed (Hutu) civilians were buried after being executed between July 27 and August 10 by government forces in the central province of Gitega.

In another report issued Thursday, UN human rights observers said 365 people (probably all Hutu) were slain in neighboring Rwanda in July. The report said 226 of the deaths were caused by 'agents of the state,' including members of the (Tutsi) Rwandan Patriotic Army, which killed 182 people during operations against Hutu insurgents. Hutu guerrillas killed 45 people, the report added, while responsibility for the deaths of the remaining 94 could not be established."[2]

Adding fuel to the fire was the revelation that high-ranking Tutsi army officers not only engineered the

114

assassination of President Ndadaye; they did so in order to keep Hutus out of power and perpetuate Tutsi domination of the country and regardless of how may Hutus were killed in the ensuing violence at the hands of Tutsi soldiers.

Although the military ruler, Major Buyoya, denied being involved in the attempted coup which resulted in Ndadaye's death, he was deeply implicated in the plot by a number of fellow Tutsis including his cousin and former president, Jean-Baptiste Bagaza; an assessment given credibility by UN investigators although they did not name him directly as a key conspirator:

"Top officers of the Burundian Army were apparently behind the 1993 assassination of the country's first Hutu president, Melchior Ndadaye, a United Nations report has concluded. 'The planning and execution of the coup was carried out by officers highly placed in the line of command of the Burundian Army,' according to the report. It was sent to the Security Council after Burundi's military ousted the government last month (25 July 1996).

According to the report, the army chief of staff, Jean Bikomagu, ordered the head of the president's bodyguards to Mauritius before the assassination and dismissed reports of unrest among military units that later staged a short-lived coup."[3]

The Tutsi-led abortive coup plunged Burundi into one of the bloodiest and one of the longest civil wars Africa has ever seen, although it went largely unreported by the international media, unlike the 1994 genocide in neighboruing Rwanda.

The killings in Burundi also amounted to genocide. While the genocide in Rwanda was carried out by the Hutu against the Tutsi, the one in Burundi was committed by the Tutsi against the Hutu. Some estimates put the death toll in Burundi's civil war – from 1993 to 1996 alone

– at 500,000, most of the victims being Hutu. One of the publications which cited this figure was *The Economist*:

"After years of bloodshed, this country, divided like Rwanda between ruling Tutsis and a Hutu majority, may well face months or years of more – and worse.

Burundi's trouble is not officially organised as genocide, as in Rwanda in 1994. Its Tutsi army was, for practical purposes, in charge even before the coup. But the killing, even if less and less publicised, has been plenty – certainly far worse than anything seen recently in Zaire....

The violence, some estimates say, may have killed 500,000 Burundians in three years."[4]

The estimates seem to be credible, given the magnitude of the conflict and the escalation of the violence, and when the statistics are looked at in another context. For example, at least 10,000 people were killed within the first eight months in 1996; more than 6,000 in three weeks alone, after the Tutsi seized power.[5]

The conflict in Burundi had all the ingredients for another Rwanda, probably with a holocaust of the same magnitude, or worse.

Compounding the problem is the fact that the two enemies are so close to each other, literally and figuratively, yet so far apart. "The two groups still live together on the same hills, share the same language (the Tutsi abandoned or lost theirs when they migrated to the region and became an integral part of the larger Hutu society), culture and economy – and still hate each other."[6]

Added to this volatile mixture was yet another element: within three years (1993 – 1996), two Hutu presidents were murdered, and the third one was forced, by the Tutsi, to seek refuge in the American embassy in Burundi's capital Bujumbura where he was holed up for a long time as if he were a fugitive from the law. Yet he fled from the very same people who broke the law by overthrowing him,

116

seizing power illegally.

This usurpation of power even angered some of Burundi's neighbours, especially Tanzania and Kenya: "Tanzania, which handles 70 per cent of Burundi's imports, including almost all its fuel, closed the border – so enthusiastically at first that food aid destined for 300,000 (mainly Hutu) refugees in Burundi was blocked."[7] It was gunboat diplomacy at its best, African style.

Although the embargo had immediate impact – petrol was severely rationed; some food prices nearly trebled; Burundi's main exports and a vital source of income for the army, coffee and tea, could no longer be exported through Tanzania – there was still skepticism about its long-term effects in terms of bringing about fundamental political change in Burundi.

This was vindicated when the sanctions failed to bring down the Tutsi military regime. Instead, violence escalated across the country, taking Burundi down the road to nowhere, except self-destruction. As former Prime Minister Adrien Sibomana poignantly stated: "(Burundi is) like a truck that has fallen into a ditch. It is a nation of people in despair."8 And the future does not look bright, as the country continues to be wracked by violence. As Thomas W. Lippman reported in *The Washington Post*:

"Hundreds of Burundians, mostly unarmed civilians, are dying daily in a conflict between the army, led by officers of the minority Tutsi tribe, and insurgent militias of the majority Hutu....

Citing intelligence reports, U.S. officials said the Tutsi-led army was preparing a nationwide campaign against armed Hutu insurgents, a campaign that could lead to large-scale killing of Hutu civilians.

At the same time, these officials said, Hutu militias appear to have received a new infusion of weapons, including heavy mortars, that they are prepared to turn against the Tutsi-populated capital city, Bujumbura.

Members of a Burundian delegation who visited New York and Washington last week (in August 1996) said there was little reason to believe the country could right itself because the level of hatred is so high and the sense of helplessness so profound."[9]

Around the same time, Burundi's ruler, Major Pierre Buyoya, attributed some of the country's plight and deteriorating situation to the economic embargo imposed by some of Burundi's neighbours, especially Tanzania and Kenya.

He warned them that the sanctions could worsen the conflict by causing a human disaster and risking further unrest. In an interview on 2 August 1996, with the Belgian daily newspaper, *Le Soir*, Buyoya said he was ready to meet Hutu opposition leaders for talks to try to build a political consensus provided "they stop behaving like mass killers, whose goal is to kill women, children and old people whose mistake is to belong to such and such an ethnic group."[10]

Yet his Tutsi army was even more notorious for committing atrocities against Hutu civilians, simply because they were Hutu, a fact he never acknowledged but instead blamed only Hutus for the murders and the violence across the country.

That is hardly a basis for meaningful dialogue, especially when he blamed only the Hutu instead of apportioning guilt accordingly. There are no saints in this war.

But it is true, as he said, that the economic embargo aggravated the situation, although the sanctions could not be blamed for the escalation of the conflict.

Hutu rebels stepped up the attacks on their own, emboldened by the sanctions in some respects but not prompted by them. And they inflicted substantial damage on some installations. For example, towards the end of August 1996, Burundi's capital was without electricity for several days straight after the rebels destroyed power facilities. And lines to buy petrol and other fuel winded through the capital Bujumbura as sabotage by Hutu rebels and the embargo began to take their toll.

The insurgents destroyed four electrical pylons on August 24th which carried power from a northern hydroelectric dam to the capital city of 400,000 people. Hutu political opponents also called on farmers – who are mostly Hutu since they constitute the vast majority of the country's population – not to deliver food to Bujumbura to protest the military coup. Even many Tutsis complied with the "order," afraid they would be targeted by the Hutu rebels if they did not.

The residents of Bujumbura, mostly Tutsi, had become increasingly angry and desperate since the sanctions were imposed a few days after the coup; a situation that worked to the advantage of the Hutu rebels but which was not enough to bring down the military regime.

Hospitals, military bases and hotels filled generators with diesel fuel which would no longer be available because of the embargo. But that was only temporary relief.

Burundi's problems – which caused the embargo, hence the shortages, in the first place – required long-term solutions. Unfortunately, it was impossible to find such solutions as long as the two ethnic groups continued to fight.

Burundi's main rebel group, the National Council for the Defence of Democracy (CNDD, a French acronym), threatened on 28 August 1996 to shoot down any aircraft flying into the nation's capital in violation of the economic embargo. CNDD spokesman, Innocent Nimpagaritse, who was also the group's East Africa representative, said in Nairobi, Kenya:

"We have information some foreign planes are landing in Bujumbura in defiance of regional sanctions. From today onwards, any plane flying into Bujumbura without clearance from our forces will be shot down."[11]

But a spokesman for Burundi's military regime, Jean-Luc Ndizeye, dismissed the Hutu threats as empty boasts:

"They don't have the technical capacity to do that, and if they do shoot a plane coming in or out of Bujumbura then it will just be another one of their crimes."[12]

During the same time, American envoy Howard Wolpe met with Tanzania's former President Julius Nyerere in Rome and proposed that Buyoya should be recognised as Burundi's president as part of a peace initiative to end the Hutu-Tutsi ethnic conflict. The two leaders met to discuss ways to end the war, and the American proposal was just one of the conceivable scenarios in which peace could be envisioned. The deal would give Major Buyoya six months to restore the National Assembly and negotiate peace between the two sides.

Nyerere held talks with Buyoya on August 25th in Tanzania as part of an effort to mediate an end to the violence. But Burundi's ambassador to Rome, Jean-Baptiste Mbonyingingo, said "the aims of the visits by Mr. Nyerere and Mr. Wolpe to Rome were not known to the Burundian government" and added that no envoys had been sent from Bujumbura to the Italian capital to deliver a message or participate in the talks.[13]

Meanwhile, the economic embargo continued to cause hardship, forcing the capital city to draw upon dwindling fuel stocks to keep water supplies, hospitals and other institutions running. Even the army itself was hit hard by the sanctions. But it continued to commit atrocities against Hutu civilians in pursuit of its scorched-earth policy of hunting down Hutu rebels and punishing their supporters, thus targeting innocent people as well.

As the violence escalated, foreigners started fleeing the

country. In the first week of September 1996, renewed fighting flared in the eastern part just outside Bujumbura, prompting the United States and other countries to evacuate their nationals from the embattled East African country. The rebels had taken the war to the capital. According to a report from Bujumbura in the *International Herald Tribune*:

"The Burundi Army was using two helicopter gunships and mortars to repel rebels in some of the fiercest fighting since the July 25 coup.

The rebels lobbed three mortar shells into the capital Tuesday (September 3) and fired rifles into the air from surrounding hills to show the Tutsi residents of Bujumbura that they could come down any time, according to a rebel spokesman."[14]

An American Air Force C-141 plane evacuated Americans and other foreigners from the besieged capital on September 4th, but Tanzania forbade it to use its airspace because of the economic embargo imposed on Burundi. Instead, the plane flew over Rwanda and Uganda to Nairobi, Kenya. With commercial flights banned and borders sealed, Burundi was virtually cut off from the rest of the world.

Shackled by the sanctions, the Tutsi military junta announced on 12 September 1996 that it was immediately lifting bans on all political parties and the National Assembly which were imposed after the coup. If genuine, the changes would have met two of the three conditions stipulated by Burundi's neighbours before lifting the embargo. But the changes were merely cosmetic.

Although Buyoya unbanned political parties, political meetings were forbidden, as were opposition newspapers. And although he reopened the parliament, where the Hutu FRODEBU party had a majority, the members met only to point out that out of 81 parliamentarians, 22 had been

121

murdered. All were FRODEBU members.

The national legislators also said they would do nothing as members of parliament until the constitution was restored.

Buyoya also agreed to unconditional peace talks with all parties, but reneged on his promise.

The third condition for lifting sanctions was unconditional peace negotiations among all parties, including the rebels. But the Hutu insurgents as well as Burundi's main Tutsi and Hutu political parties dismissed the lifting of political bans as a move to loosen the sanctions.

Charles Mukasi, leader of the Tutsi UPRONA party, said lifting bans was meaningless because Burundi's parliament had no real power even before the coup, and would stay powerless. He went on to say, "lifting the ban on Parliament is a cosmetic change simply designed to please Nyerere"[15] who initiated and coordinated the regional sanctions against the impoverished landlocked nation.

What the Tutsi rulers deliberately refused to address was the inequity of power between the two ethnic groups; a conflict deeply rooted in history. Instead, like their ethnic compatriots in Rwanda, they were determined to perpetuate their hegemonic control over the Hutu majority, with dire consequences for the entire region which has literally been engulfed in flames.

The biggest catalyst in this inferno is ethno-nationalism, probably the most potent force in the world today which could change the map of Africa in the twentieth-first century, as it did in Eastern Europe and in the Soviet Union after the collapse of communism towards the end of the twentieth century. As Professor William Zartman stated in his article, "Making Sense of East Africa's Wars," in *The Wall Street Journal*:

"The current round in the unfolding Central African

crisis is the result of three countries' (Rwanda's, Burundi's, and Zaire's) attempts at national consolidation on an ethnic basis – the same type of dynamic that has been driving civil wars in the former Yugoslavia (especially Bosnia and Kosovo) and the former Soviet Union (especially Tajikistan."[16]

The intensity of such micro-nationalism in the Great Lakes region has another dimension which makes it even more potent because it is articulated in a "racial" context, although it defies rational explanation contending that the Hutu and the Tutsi belong to different races. And it is sanctioned by the state – the Tutsi ethnocracy – which, by its actions, glorifies it as a virtue at the expense of pluralistic aspirations a heterogeneous society is expected to pursue in order to accommodate its diverse elements on the basis of equality. And tragically, the history of both Rwanda and Burundi is a chronicle of the tribulations of a people divided purely on the basis of what they are or what they perceive themselves to be. But the divisions are real, as are the inequities. As *The Economist* states:

"The relationship between Hutus and Tutsis goes deep into history. It was not always so clear-cut – or deadly.
Hutus tell of centuries of enslavement by Tutsis. Tutsis say that the ethnic divide was invented by colonial rulers, and that Hutus are playing racial politics.
Anyone on the watch for it – and these days everyone is – can spot the difference between Hutu and Tutsi stereotypes. Line up ten people, five Tutsis and five Hutus. The ethnic origin of six would be plain, two could be either, two you would get wrong. Intermarriage has lessened the physical differences; politicians have built up the emotional ones, making the division even sharper than before."[17]

Superficial as they may be in some respects, the

differences are real in a very deadly way. That is why almost 1 million Tutsis were slaughtered in Rwanda. Their Hutu enemies did not miss their target – in most cases, they knew who to go after, based on physical features or appearance alone.

They were able to identify Tutsis right away, sometimes even by looking at the shape of their heels (if it was L-shaped, without a curve, "you are Tutsi!"), or at their gums (if they are dark, "you are Tutsi!").

Employing such criteria is indeed arbitrary. But in most cases, they were right on target. Otherwise they would have killed a very large number of their own people, had they simply guessed who was Tutsi and who was not, although they probably also killed an unknown number of fellow Hutus whom they mistook for Tutsis. But probably the most important factor was that they knew the people they killed. They killed their neighbours. They killed their friends and even their own relatives. And they already knew they were Tutsi.

The differences between the two groups are also real in a fundamental respect: allocation of power, hence resources.

It is the Tutsi who dominate. They control the army; they control the government, the economy and everything else. Those who rule set the rules of the game. When their opponents learn the game, they change the rules.

In Burundi, such hegemonic control by the Tutsi has included not only discrimination in the provision of education but also extermination of the Hutu elite, resulting in the intellectual suffocation of an entire people, with appalling results: "If you hire educated people in Burundi's towns these days (in the late 1990s), you hire Tutsis. The divide has become absolute."[18] Therefore the Hutu-Tutsi conflict is also a class conflict.

It is also political because the Hutu are excluded from power; it is also economic, mainly a conflict over land of which there is so little for so many people; and it is, of course, "racial": Nilotic (Tutsi) versus Bantu (Hutu), although there is no Bantu race. Bantus themselves – united only by linguistic affinity and cultural similarities – are different peoples; they are not just one people.

But the Hutu-Tutsi ethnic divide has no parallel in the region. The schism is so wide, and so frightening. Prospects are bleak we will see it closed in the next several decades. It probably never will be. And both sides know that.

What we will probably see in both countries is a *façade* of democracy, accommodating both groups on "equal basis," while in reality one group or the other will always be dominant, exercising power to preserve, protect and promote its own interests at the expense of the other group.

The Tutsi don't want to share – let alone relinquish – power. And the Hutu, once in power as they once were in Rwanda from 1962 to 1994, will probably rule forever if democracy is established on the basis of majority rule. They constitute the vast majority of the population in both countries and are therefore guaranteed to win every election even without rigging. The election of Melchior Ndadaye, a Hutu, in 1993 as president of Burundi clearly demonstrated that. He rode into office on a massive wave of Hutu sentiment, sending shivers down the spine of many Tutsis, probably the majority of them.

It is a cruel dilemma which explains why the two ethnic groups are locked in perpetual conflict.

The search for a solution to this intra-territorial conflict is analogous to the quest for peace and stability in the global arena where equilibrium in the international system is determined by one of two things: domination by one power or by a group of powers united by common interests; or peaceful coexistence between global adversaries. The alternative is chaos.

In the case of Rwanda and Burundi, domination of one group by the other has failed to bring peace. Peaceful

125

coexistence between the two groups within the same national boundaries has also failed. The result has been war, chaos and anarchy.

War versus Diplomacy

The Tutsi soldiers who seized power from a Hutu president in Burundi in July 1996 only heightened fear among the Hutu that the Tutsi were not interested in peaceful coexistence or power sharing. They clearly showed that they were interested in dominating the Hutu. This led to escalation of the conflict which reached new levels in December the same year, five months after the coup.[19]

And there was mounting evidence showing that the Tutsi national army was waging a vicious campaign of terror against Hutu civilians. The United Nations High Commissioner for Human Rights, Jose Ayala Lasso, gave the evidence on 11 December 1996 showing that Burundi's army had killed at least 1,100 people in two months, including hundreds of Hutu refugees, and urged the country's Tutsi leaders to stop the carnage:

"I appeal to the authorities and all parties to ensure maximum respect for human rights and fundamental freedoms to put an end to killings, arbitrary arrests, destruction of property."[20]

The report, based on UN investigations and testimony by witnesses, said the massacres had taken place in October and November 1996.

The UN human rights office said the biggest massacre during that period took place when Tutsi soldiers killed 200 to 400 Hutu returnees and wounded 200 others in an attack on a church in the village of Murambi in the northwestern province of Citiboke.

The report also stated that Hutu rebels fighting the army may have killed scores of civilians. And it warned that an already alarming situation had been made worse by the influx of more than 50,000 Burundian Hutu refugees who fled a rebellion by the Banyamulenge and other Tutsis – including Rwandan and Burundian Tutsi soldiers – in eastern Zaire.

Killings, disappearances and arbitrary arrests had risen sharply in Burundi since the influx began. The UN report went on state that civilians – mostly Hutu – were bearing the brunt of the increasingly violent confrontations between Tutsi soldiers and Hutu rebels, with the insurgents using mortars and the army striking with planes:

"The human rights situation in November (1996) could be described as alarming, with massacres, arbitrary arrests, pillage and destruction of property perpetrated by the two sides."[21]

But the Tutsi army wreaked more havoc in its campaign of state-sponsored terrorism against the Hutu. The war also amounted to ethnic cleansing. According to a report from Burundi by *The Economist*:

"Burundi's soldiers have been fighting Hutu guerrillas in a war of terror and counter-terror, with few scruples on either side.

By now much of the northern countryside, if not already guerrilla-controlled, is open to guerrilla attack. Many Tutsis have fled to the towns; often Hutus have fled or been pushed out from them (including the capital Bujumbura which was cleansed of almost all Hutus by the Tutsi)."[22]

The deterioration of the situation was underscored by the promulgation of two decrees in December 1996 which pointed to a bleak future.

One stated that all school leavers and public employees must do a year's army service and be available for "public works," a term whose meaning needed no further explanation in the military language of conscription.

The other decree required all public employees to contribute a month's salary to the military campaign, and all employers to give workers time off for army service.

Burundi's military regime further demonstrated its commitment to a military solution to the ethnic conflict when it refused to participate in peace talks. When Julius Nyerere, the chief mediator in the Burundi conflict, invited the Tutsi military ruler to attend a meeting of all parties in Tanzania in the last week of December 1996, "Mr. Buyoya did not even reply."[23] As one diplomat put it: "This is a complete militarisation of society. They are determined to squash the rebellion."[24]

But this uncompromising stand only fuelled the conflict.

In the first week of December 1996, up to 500 people were killed in attacks in Kayanza Province north of the capital Bujumbura. The killings were attributed to both – Hutu rebels and Tutsi soldiers.

The Tutsi army intensified its campaign when it resorted to resettlement schemes, forcing Hutu peasants to leave their homes and farms and settle in "protective" villages which were no more than concentration camps reminiscent of what the British did in Malaya during the 1950s, and what the Americans did in South Vietnam in the 1960s.

The Tutsi regime claimed that Hutu peasants in war-torn areas were moved to other parts "for their own safety." That was a cruel joke by the regime which was busy killing the same people it claimed it was protecting. Most of the Hutu civilians who were killed – were killed by the Tutsi army, not by the Hutu rebels.

The real motive for moving Hutu peasants into so-called protective villages or areas was to deprive Hutu guerrilla fighters of civilian support from their people, fellow Hutus, and to hold Hutu civilians hostage – in "protective" villages – in retaliation for attacks by Hutu insurgents on Tutsi civilians and soldiers. For every Tutsi killed, so many Hutus would be killed in the concentration camps. Any Hutu who did not relocate or move into a "protective" village was automatically considered to be a rebel and fair game for Tutsi soldiers.

The army was free to do anything it wanted to do because it was the most powerful institution in the country. And it still is.

Even if its leader Pierre Buyoya, the military head of state, wanted to negotiate with the rebels, he would not have been able to do so without army support. As one observer put it: "If he negotiates with the Hutu rebels, he's a dead man."[25]

But it seemed that even he himself had opted for a military solution to the problem even if the army did not exert pressure on him to adopt an uncompromising stand against the peace talks. That is because he thought he could win the war, especially with the isolation of the rebels from their civilian supporters under his resettlement programme which ended up creating some of the most notorious concentration camps on the African continent reminiscent of what happened in Kenya in the 1950s during Mau Mau when tens of thousands of Kikuyus were penned up in barren reserves by the British.

Another reason why Buyoya thought the Tutsi army would win the war had to do with what had just happened right next-door. The Banyamulenge Tutsis in eastern Zaire had just routed the Burundian and Rwandan Hutu guerrillas who had operational bases in that part of Congo, posing great danger to the Tutsi regimes in both Rwanda and Burundi. With the destruction of their operational bases, he felt that this danger had been eliminated or had been greatly reduced, making it difficult for the insurgents to launch raids into Burundi from their bases in Zaire.

He also believed that his army could duplicate this success within Burundi itself, considering its performance through the years as a better fighting force than the rebels. But he also underestimated the rebels.

It is true that, more often than not, the Tutsi have demonstrated great ability on the battlefield and have always been proud of their military prowess. And the record speaks for itself, not only in Burundi but also in Rwanda as was clearly demonstrated during the 1994 genocide when the Hutu army was routed by the Tutsi insurgents of the Rwandan Patriotic Front (RPF).

Yet they have not always prevailed against the Hutu even in Burundi itself. The Hutu also turned the tables in Rwanda, first during the 1959 mass uprising in which they ousted the Tutsi aristocracy and killed more than 100,000 Tutsis, forcing hundreds of thousands of others to flee the country; and again in 1994 when they almost wiped out the entire Tutsi population in Rwanda in an unprecedented genocide which claimed about one million lives.

Buyoya was also encouraged to pursue a military solution because the economic embargo which had inflicted a lot of pain on the army as well, was now being circumvented.

But it was a war neither side could win, although the sanction-busters, mostly Francophone African countries sympathetic to another French-speaking country in plight, encouraged the Tutsi military regime in its belief that it could:

"Times are tough: fuel prices have risen sixfold, and building has all but stopped for lack of cement. But there is food in the markets and enough fuel is smuggled from Rwanda to allow life to go on and the army to fight.

The government has been encouraged by feelings building up in French-speaking Africa against sanctions. Sympathy for Mr. Buyoya was plain at two recent high-level meetings (in December 1996) in Congo (Brazzaville) and Burkina Faso; one brought calls for the sanctions to be eased.

The government is losing its former coffee revenues, but, with eastern Zaire's airports now in Tutsi rebel hands, exports may get out by that route (as well as through Rwanda, with Burundi's coffee and tea bags labelled as Rwanda's exports).

With little chance of a political breakthrough, the pattern of war is likely to continue. Hutu fighters attack a school or health clinic, or some group of displaced Tutsi families. The (Tutsi) army moves in, burns (Hutu) villages and murders whatever unlucky Hutus it comes upon. Neither side can win."[26]

And neither side is going to surrender, as the escalation of violence clearly shows.

Yet these are the people who have lived together and who have intermarried through the years, in fact for centuries, without plunging their country into massive violence, until after independence in the sixties.

There had always been hostility between the two groups since the Tutsi conquered and virtually enslaved the Hutu about 400 years ago. But in all those years, the conflict never reached the levels it did from the 1960s to the 1990s.

What went wrong?

The injustices against the Hutu through the centuries undoubtedly had cumulative impact which contributed to the eruption of violence on an unprecedented scale during that period – from the sixties to the nineties. But something else played a role: Hutu politicians and intellectuals with warped minds whipping up"racist" or ethnic sentiments against the Tutsi. As Julius Nyerere stated in his speech to the International Peace Academy in New York in January 1997:

"All violent conditions represent earlier failures of

leadership, either by wrongdoing or by default. They represent failures at local levels, and especially at national levels....

In Africa today, and especially in Rwanda and Burundi, we hear a great deal about ethnic conflicts. Yet these are taking place at particular times and places after members of the different ethnic groups have for long periods lived side by side in the same villages and towns, have worked together and have intermarried. Thus, ethnicity is clearly not a sufficient explanation of conflict.

Ethnicity can, however, be used to conceal the real problems, the genuine economic problems or cultural clashes, behind the easily aroused human fears about those who are unlike ourselves. Ethnicity can also be used to divide and rule. In Rwanda and Burundi, this use of ethnicity was clearly made by Germany and Belgium as colonial powers.

Ethnic conflict will arise when leaders in the society deliberately strengthen the concept of ethnicity, and for their own purposes ignite hostility. In Rwanda and Burundi, conflict has economic roots. The fight for power is mainly a fight for economic resources. Ethnicity is simply being exploited."[27]

The Tutsi control both political power and economic resources. Yet such politics of exclusion will not guarantee security even for the Tutsi themselves in spite of all the power they have. In fact, it has made most Tutsis vulnerable to attack since everyone of them symbolises oppression of the Hutu. That is the way Hutu rebels and their supporters see it.

Therefore every Tutsi, everyone of them, is a target everywhere, not by every Hutu but by Hutu rebels and by other Hutus who use violence against their enemies or against those whom they perceive to be their enemies. And no amount of security by the Tutsi army is going to be enough to protect every Tutsi, in every part of the country, all the time, as the killings of Tutsi civilians by Hutu insurgents tragically demonstrates.

Yet it is this very threat to their survival which Tutsis invoke to justify their determination to hang on to power at any cost and by any means at their disposal including the use of deadly force against any Hutu they think is a threat to them. And that includes innocent civilians who are considered to be dangerous simply because they are Hutu.

It is this threat to Tutsi survival which also compelled the Tutsi military ruler, Major Pierre Buyoya, to start talking to the rebels. And history bears testimony to one brutal fact: It was in Burundi where the Great Lakes crisis started when Tutsi soldiers assassinated the country's first democratically elected president, a Hutu, in 1993, starting a bloodbath which spilled throughout the region and alerted the Hutu in Rwanda as to what would happen to them if the Tutsi also seized power in that country.

The ethnic conflict in both Rwanda and Burundi not only caused more than one million deaths – probably one-and-a-half million – in four years since 1993; it also ignited hostilities between the governments of neighbouring countries and others even further from the region; it displaced millions of people; disrupted trade among the countries in the region and weakened their economies; and plunged the entire region into chaos on an unprecedented scale.

Therefore resolution of the conflict was of paramount concern on the agenda of several countries in the region which wanted to extricate themselves from the imbroglio, as much as it was even for many people in Burundi who felt that neither side could win the war.

In anticipation of the peace negotiations scheduled for September 1997 in neighbouring Tanzania, Buyoya said in an interview in August that the talks could lead to the establishment of a coalition government acceptable to the Tutsi minority. As he put it:

"Democracy is possible, but we have to reinvent our democracy, a democracy adapted to Burundi's realities, that would take into account our culture and experience, our social and political reality. We have to adapt democracy to what we are."[28]

But it was also obvious that a comprehensive peace agreement by Buyoya could cost him his life. That is because he was put in power by Tutsi business leaders and military officers who had the most to lose if the Tutsi relinquished control and democracy was re-established, leading to the election of a Hutu president; which was a virtual certainty, given the tyranny of numbers tipping scales in favour Hutus in this deeply divided country where most people automatically vote along ethnic lines.

Buyoya himself admitted that he probably would be overthrown – and much worse – if he endorsed any peace accord which did not guarantee the Tutsi elite's hold on influence and financial advantage: "I will try to bring a peace accord without causing a coup. You have to manage it so the Burundi people, including the military, are part of the accord."[29]

That is in a country where the Tutsi savagely repressed Hutu uprisings in 1963, 1965, 1972, 1988, 1991, and 1993, at a cost of at least one million lives, mostly Hutu; a holocaust – of several genocides through the years – hardly anyone talks about unlike the 1994 tragedy that befell the Tutsi in Rwanda. It is this kind of disregard for their plight by the international community and by their fellow countrymen, the Tutsi, which rankles the Hutu in Burundi. Throughout this horrendous tragedy, they have largely remained an invisible mass unlike their kinsmen, and unlike the Tutsi, in Rwanda.

Therefore to ask Hutus in Burundi to continue living under Tutsi domination would be equivalent to asking black people in South Africa during the apartheid era to continue enduring white oppression without demanding fundamental change and a complete overhaul of the system.

Yet democracy on the basis of "one man, one vote" is not a realistic solution to the ethnic conflict in Burundi – or Rwanda – because the Tutsi see it as a recipe for catastrophe, leading to genocide against them by the victorious Hutus.

It is difficult to conceive of a scenario in which the Hutu lose an election on the basis of one man, one vote. As Charles Mukasi, the secretary-general of Burundi's Tutsi ruling party, UPRONA, bluntly stated:

"The Tutsi are not scared of elections. They are scared of being exterminated."[30]

The Hutu are not scared of elections, either. And they may not even be scared of being exterminated because there are so many of them, vastly outnumbering the Tutsi. But they are scared of being dominated and of being massacred by the Tutsi.

Both groups have legitimate fears vindicated by history.

But in spite of the hostility and deep resentment between the two groups, each united by fear of the other, neither the Hutu nor the Tutsi always present a united front in pursuit of their goals as ethnic entities. This was best demonstrated during the late 1990s when attempts were made to resolve the ethnic conflict.

There were Tutsi moderates who supported Buyoya's peace initiative, and hawks who were vehemently opposed to it. Hutus were also divided along the same lines.

And although the Hutu rebels were united by their common hatred of the Tutsi, there were times when they also clashed among themselves. One of the worst clashes took place in northwestern Burundi where fighting between rival Hutu insurgents between July and August

1997 left 600 people dead.

In mid-August 1997, about 13,000 Hutus fled their rural homes and sought refuge in Bubanza, a trading town 25 miles north of the capital Bujumbura, to escape fighting between two Hutu guerrilla groups – the National Liberation Front (FROLINA) and the Forces for the Defence of Democracy (FDD) which was the main guerrilla group in Burundi.

A farmer who arrived in a town nearby said many villagers were fleeing because the National Liberation Front "will kill us if we don't give them financial support." A spokesman for the National Council for the Defence of Democracy (CNDD), the political wing of the FDD, denied that factional fighting caused the deaths.[31]

But more than one witness confirmed the fighting. And there was evidence showing that it took place.

However, none of these intra-ethnic conflicts distracted the insurgents from their common goal of trying to oust the Tutsi from power.

But the rebels also targeted their own people, fellow Hutus, for different reasons. Not all Hutus supported the rebels. And not all Hutus believed violence was the solution to the ethnic problem in Burundi. Hutus opposed to guerrilla war were prime targets. Others were killed in raids for food and shelter. Yet others were taken hostage and used as human shields; Tutsi soldiers showed little concern for them.

To them, every Hutu was fair game, and hostages an expendable commodity or just a part of collateral damage, as they carried on their campaign of brutal repression and indiscriminate killings ostensibly to destroy Hutu guerrillas. Anything in their way, including Hutu hostages, was prime target; every Hutu a suspect, to be harassed or arrested, tortured or killed, or interned in a concentration camp.

The plight of one Hutu community of Buraniro illustrates the tragedy that had befallen the rest of their kinsmen in general at the hands of their Tutsi rulers. But it is also a story about the atrocities committed by the rebels themselves against their own people.

Like most Hutus, Mrs. Mary Rose Habyamberi lived in a banana-leaf hut, scratching out a bare living on a plot of land, growing food crops including bananas and vegetables. Yet in the midst of war, poverty was the least of her worries. She was, instead, afraid of the heavily-armed Tutsi soldiers who patrolled around the camp where she had been interned with other Hutus and kept under intense watch.

But she was also scared of the Hutu guerrillas roaming the hills of this densely-populated mountainous country.

In the latter part of 1996, the guerrillas raided for supplies the commune where she lived, killing several people in a hail of gunfire. Among those killed was her 10-year-old son, Olivier. As she sadly recalled in an interview almost a year later in August 1997: "They killed my child. He was fleeing and I never saw him again."[32]

Mrs. Habyamberi became a victim of both sides. But the vast majority of Hutus who were forced into "protective" camps were mostly victims of a vicious campaign by Tutsi soldiers against the Hutu guerrillas.

Mrs. Mary Rose Habyamberi was one of the 13,000 Hutus who had been forced out of their villages by Tutsi soldiers and crowded into a concentration camp around the trading post of Buraniro as part of a scorched-earth policy by President Buyoya's government to neutralise the insurgents.

In August 1997, human rights workers and aid officials said there were at least 44 camps like the one at Buraniro, across Burundi, with about 255,000 people living in appalling conditions. But they also, together with diplomats, conceded that forcing Hutu peasants into the camps had been a successful military strategy. It robbed the guerrillas of supply lines and hiding places, and made it harder for them to recruit young men into the guerrilla force. As Buyoya stated, in justifying this policy: "We are obliged to regroup people to protect them. We have to put them somewhere where they can live together in security."[33]

But the people living in the camps disagreed with that glossy assessment. Life for them was hard. Although some were allowed to go back to their farms during daylight hours, many of them missed the planting season. Even those who had been able to plant could work on their farms for only a few hours a day, thus severely reducing the harvest. Many of them said they were expecting less than half of their normal harvest of yams, cassava and beans.

Therefore, while the concentration-camp policy benefited the military, it also caused famine conditions for Hutu peasants.

But it was a policy not without precedent even in Africa itself. And it was effective.

Hunger has been used effectively as a weapon in many wars to starve people into submission. It was used by the federal military government in the Nigerian civil war to force the Biafran secessionists to capitulate. It was used by UNITA rebels in Angola to try and turn the people against the MPLA government, hoping that they would rise up in a mass insurrection to compel the national leadership to make substantial concessions to the rebels on terms stipulated by UNITA.

Hunger was also used by the brutal regime of Mengistu Haile Mariam in Ethiopia against the peasants opposed to his reign of terror, and by Siad Barre, another brutal despot, in Somalia whose tyranny destroyed the country – it dissolved in anarchy.

Hunger was also one of the weapons – in addition to chopping off limbs, buttocks and ears as well as gouging out eyes – the rebels of the Revolutionary United Front (RUF) used in Sierra Leone to wage war against the democratically elected government of President Ahmad

Tejan Kabbah, although the grisly mutilations and amputations played a bigger role.

President Kabbah was forced to seek peace literally on the rebels' terms which included making the RUF leader, Foday Sankoh, vice president of Sierra Leone, and giving eight ministerial posts – four of which were deputy ministerial – to the RUF rebels and their allies: renegade soldiers who overthrew Kabbah in May 1997. He was reinstated in March 1998 with the help of the West African peacekeeping force (ECOMOG) led by Nigeria.

The difference in Burundi is that it was the Tutsi-dominated military regime which dictated terms to the Hutu majority. Forcing them to live in concentrations camps – or die – was one of those terms. In addition to being interned, the people in the camps were also forced to live in squalid conditions without sanitation. There were hardly any latrines; there was no clean water, not enough food, and much more:

"People...are living on top of one another. Disease is rampant: typhoid fever, dysentery and malaria. And with limited harvests, malnutrition is beginning to take hold in some camps, aid workers said."[34]

The Tutsi military regime painted an entirely different picture. And it continued to say the camps were created to provide security and isolate the rebels who were attacking Hutu civilians as well. Yet hardly any of the interned Hutus said they moved into the camps willingly. Anyone – any Hutu – caught outside the camps at night was automatically considered to be a rebel and could be shot on sight.

There was another intimidating aspect of life in those places which made them qualify as concentration camps. Although none had barbed wire fences or guard towers, they were all garrisoned by Tutsi soldiers in order to prevent the people from leaving the camps.

139

If the Hutu peasants had settled in the camps willingly or voluntarily, there would have been no need for all those soldiers to be on the premises, worried about Hutus escaping from the so-called protective villages.

Buraniro was one of the few places where people were allowed to return to their farms during the day. In the rest of the camps, Hutu peasants were forced to work collectively on a single tract of land at a time, almost like a prison chain gang. And in some camps, the people couldn't leave at all, because of security problems, the soldiers claimed. Yet nobody, not even the soldiers themselves, was convinced or believed this was really the reason the Hutus were confined to the camps.

The plight of the interned Hutu peasants was highlighted by the predicament of one such farmer, Marcel Nyabenda, a 50-year-old father of nine children, at Buraniro.

His farm was a two-hour walk away, and he had to be back in the camp by 6 P.M., hardly enough time for him to work on the farm. By the time he got there, he was already tired from walking, therefore unable to work as hard as he normally would have. His problem, like that of the other peasants, was compounded by the fact that he was weak from malnutrition and rampant disease in the crowded camp.

His situation got even worse when the Tutsi soldiers guarding the camp did not even allow him to go to his farm in February (1997), the last planting days; many other farmers were not allowed, either. As he explained his plight: "This time I will not harvest because I didn't cultivate."[35]

He went on to explain that he would not dare return to his farm permanently because Tutsi soldiers would shoot him as "a rebel." And the tragedy that had befallen his family as a result of this forced resettlement was enormous.

Since January 1997 when he and other Hutus from his

140

community of Nyabibuye were moved into the camp, his brother, mother and father died from typhus, one of the diseases endemic in those filthy, highly congested "security" enclaves.

But there were a few Hutus who said they were glad to be in the camps. They said they no longer had to worry about being attacked by the rebels who tortured or killed fellow Hutus who did not support their guerrilla campaign. Anyone who refused to join their guerrilla army or who did not give them food and shelter was fair game.

Ancilla Ndayisenga, a 20-year-old, was one of the residents who was grateful to the government for being given "sanctuary" in the Buraniro "protective" camp: "I like staying here. The rebels find us at our houses and attack us, so the soldiers ask us to come here and protect us."[36]

But the vast majority of the Hutus who were forced to live in the concentration camps did not share that view. Otherwise, they would have moved there willingly.

And from a humanitarian point of view, human rights workers, diplomats and UN officials said forcing people to live in the camps was indefensible regardless of how much the Tutsi regime tried to justify the internment on security grounds. But it is also true that since the military ruler, Buyoya, began moving more and more people into the camps in early 1997, security in the northern and central provinces improved significantly.

By August, the insurgency was confined to the southern part of the country near the border with Tanzania where the rebels used UN refugee camps in western Tanzania as operational bases from which to launch sporadic raids into Burundi.

President Buyoya also enlarged the Tutsi army from 17,000 to 40,000 soldiers, filling the main roads and secondary routes with heavily-armed troops. And in the camps themselves, the military regime launched a propaganda campaign to try to convince Hutu peasants

141

that the Tutsi army was not their enemy but their ally against a common enemy: the rebels.

But none of those tactics – intimidation and internment of Hutus in concentration camps, and indoctrination – helped the army to win the war. As one UN official said dismissively about the anti-rebel propaganda in the camps by the government: "What they are doing in the camps is really brainwashing."[37]

Al that probably only drove many interned Hutus even deeper into the rebels' camp even if they could not then support the rebels' cause with material assistance. As some Hutu peasants – they had not yet been rounded up and put in concentration camps by the Tutsi army – stated in Burarana in northern Burundi in October 1996 when asked in an interview with *The Economist* what caused their misfortune, forcing them to beg for food from the UN World Food Programme, handed out to them by – of all people, as the Hutu saw it – their enemies, the Tutsi, whom they hated and feared:

"The army did this, they chased us from our homes and killed people."

And the rebels?: "Yes, they take our things and our food, but they are our sons, we support them."[38]

In its special report from Burundi, *The Economist* summed up the plight of these huddled masses in the following terms:

"From a distance it looks like a market day. Some 3,000 people are gathered around three small lorries parked on the red earth road at a bend in the narrow valley. Ths is Burarana in northern Burundi.

The trucks, hired by the United Nations World Food Programme, are piled with white sacks of flour.

More people are filing down the steep hillsides to join the crowd; women in bright wraps with babies on their backs, old men with walking sticks. Come closer and you notice that they have a huddled look to them, their own apparel worn and torn. They are afraid. They are Hutus.

A few days earlier, Hutu rebels came through the area. They took food from the people. A day later, Burundi's (Tutsi) army arrived, shot and beat people and burned their huts....The survivors fled towards Burarana. Some have found space in the huts of relatives or friends, others sleep in the open....

The UN workers supervising the unloading of the food are anxious to get going....Three soldiers guard this delivery. All are tall and light-skinned. So are the UN workers supervising the unloading. These are townspeople, dressed in smart jeans and sporting flashy watches. All are Tutsis. Some carry switches to keep back the hungry (Hutu) peasants who need the food but regard its distributors with fear and loathing....

What will these people do now? They shrug. Their homes have been looted and destroyed. They have joined the mass of hungry, homeless humanity, escaping gunfire, seeking food.

There are millions of such people now in Africa's Great Lakes region. Soon there will be many millions more.

The whole region is smouldering. Eastern Zaire has now ignited, catching fire from Rwanda and Burundi. The conflagration threatens to spread even further, even to Uganda and western Tanzania. Eventually, it could affect more than 30 million people."[39]

It did affect all of Rwanda and Burundi where it all started. It affected the entire Congo (formerly Zaire) where Rwandan and Burundian Hutus sought refuge, and when the Tutsi-led rebellion which began in the eastern part of Zaire swept across the country and eventually ousted President Mobutu Sese Seko. It also affected Tanzania where hundreds of thousands of Hutu refugees – and many Tutsis – from both Rwanda and Burundi, and tens of thousands of refugees who fled from the war in Congo, settled in the western part of the country.

They were concentrated in the western regions of Tanzania along the border with the three countries – Rwanda, Burundi, and Congo – which had just exploded, affecting millions of people in the Great Lakes region.

It also affected Uganda where explosions in Rwanda, Burundi, and Congo fuelled anti-government rebellions.

And the fires have not died anywhere in the region. For example, the multinational war in Congo – involving armies from nine African countries – which started in August 1998 in the eastern part of the country and which almost stopped after all the parties involved signed a peace agreement in July 1999, reignited, full-scale, only a few months later in November. According to *The Christian Science Monitor*:

"The fragile four-month-old peace in Congo appeared over as leaders of rival rebel movements said their forces were resuming efforts to topple President Laurent Kabila.

The Congolese Liberation Movement accused Kabila's troops of attacking its positions Friday (5 November 1999) and of using the period since the signing of a truce in July to rearm.

The Congolese Rally for Democracy also said it no longer would observe the truce.

UN experts have been in Congo since October 13 to draw up plans for a peacekeeping mission."[40]

And Burundi's war, which is the least reported, is one of the most protracted and deadliest conflicts on the entire continent in the post-colonial period. The military solution being pursued by both sides to solve this intractable problem not only perpetuates but exacerbates the conflict.

That is one of the reasons – favouring a military solution – why Burundi's Tutsi military regime refused to participate in the peace negotiations in Arusha, Tanzania, in August 1997, despite Buyoya's promise that he would.

The talks began on August 26th when Nyerere, the chief mediator, said he would go on with the meeting despite Buyoya's refusal to take part in the negotiations. Nyerere also dismissed as "stupid" accusations that he was pro-Hutu and therefore unacceptable as a facilitator of the peace process.

Burundi claimed that Tanzania's neutrality had been compromised because it harboured Hutu rebels along its western border. Nyerere was blunt in his response to accusations that he favoured Hutus: "These accusations are not new. These are stupid reasons."[41]

The former Tanzanian president held talks with the representatives of the main Hutu rebel organisation, the National Council for the Defence of Democracy (CNDD); the main Hutu political party, FRODEBU; the radical Tutsi party, PARENA; and two other political parties. But without the participation of the Tutsi military regime, it was obvious that the conflict could not be resolved.

And while the war was going on in Burundi, tensions between Tanzania and Burundi also flared up and escalated into a fiery exchange, although neither side claimed or admitted responsibility for firing first:

"Tanzania was accused of firing across its border at military positions inside Burundi (in October 1997). A Burundi Army spokesman said Tanzanian forces shelled Mugina and Kabonga, killing two soldiers and wounding three others.

Tanzania's Foreign Ministry said it was unaware of any violence.

The two nation's relations have deteriorated in recent months."[42]

Burundi's conflict with Tanzania had to do with failure of leadership within Burundi itself to accommodate and protect the interests of the Hutu majority. Otherwise there would have been no need for Hutus to flee their homeland. And there would have been no Hutu refugees in Tanzania – hundreds of thousands of them. They fled the war which the Tutsi themselves started when they assassinated the country's first democratically elected president, Melchior Ndadaye, a Hutu, in order to perpetuate their hegemonic control of the country.

And their cross-border raids into Tanzania in pursuit of the Hutu rebels inevitably triggered a military response from Tanzania after diplomatic efforts failed to restrain Burundi's Tutsi army from striking across the border, forcing more refugees to flee to Tanzania because of its relentless and extremely brutal repression of the Hutu majority.

It is in this context that Tanzania's retaliatory response must be viewed. The military response was also a warning to the Tutsi military regime in Burundi to desist from launching further provocative attacks on its eastern neighbour. It is also in this context that stepped-up attacks by Hutu insurgents against Burundi's military junta must be looked at as a legitimate response to brutal oppression of the Hutu majority by the dominant Tutsi minority; even if some of their methods, including indiscriminate killings, can not be justified.

But their determination to continue fighting must also be viewed in the overall context of a system of government whose sole existence is on predicated on the politics of exclusion to perpetuate a Tutsi ethnocracy, and not as a savage instinct or morbid desire by the Hutu to exterminate members of a different "race" or ethnic group who "simply don't belong here."

It all boils down to injustice. Unless this injustice is addressed across the spectrum to accommodate conflicting interests of both groups, there will be no peace in Burundi. And the Hutu majority know there is strength in numbers even if the ruling Tutsi minority, blinded by a twisted sense of "racial" superiority, try to ignore this simple

146

reality simply because they have dominated the Hutu for hundreds of years; thus automatically assuming that they have the divine right to rule them.

But it is only a matter of time. They are not going to rule forever. And it will be a horrendous tragedy if the only way they will be compelled to face reality is by force, not by logic. We don't need another holocaust.

Intensified Guerrilla Warfare

Efforts by Hutu rebels to dislodge the Tutsi from power reached a new level on New Year's day in 1998 when the insurgents launched their biggest attack just outside the capital, Bujumbura, since the latest war began in October 1993 following the assassination of President Melchior Ndadaye in that month.

About 1,000 Hutu guerrillas attacked an army base and a village near Bujumbura airport. They fought an hour-long battle in which at least 150 civilians were killed. Colonel Jean-Bosco Darangwe, the commander of the army base, described the attack as the biggest by the Hutu rebels.

He went on to say that the rebels launched the attack as part of a broader and coordinated strategy to destabilise the governments of Burundi, Rwanda, and the Democratic Republic of Congo (DRC). The three countries were then allies against the insurgents until Congo under President Laurent Kabila switched sides in August 1998 when Rwanda, Uganda, and Burundi invaded his country in an attempt to overthrow him.

Colonel Darangwe also said the rebels were pillaging villages as they retreated: "They are attacking anything on their way out. They are killing indiscriminately be it Hutu or Tutsi. They are also forcefully taking people with them as they retreat."[43] But the rebels blamed the army for the massacre.[44]

The army beat back the assault after hours of heavy artillery fire. Lieutenant-Colonel Mamert Sinaranzi told Radio Burundi that 30 rebels and two soldiers were also killed in addition to the civilian casualties.[45]

The rebels retreated north through Rukaramu village, embroiling villagers in the fighting.

Burundi's ambassador to Britain, Jean-Luc Ndizye, said 150 civilian victims were Hutu, like the rebels, and were killed in Rukaramu.[46] But it was not clear who killed the villagers: Hutu rebels or Tutsi soldiers. Bodies of the victims were strewn in the fields of the community.

In the past, Hutu guerrillas have killed Hutu civilians suspected of not supporting their cause. But most of those attacks have been organised strikes on specific locations. However, in the attack on Rukaramu, it appeared that the villagers happened to be in the path of the rebels' retreat.[47] And although rebels regularly strike in northwestern and southern Burundi, two Hutu strongholds, the New Year's attack was the first one on a military target near the capital in two years.

Colonel Darangwe said the army was still finding wounded villagers, and that the death toll could rise as soldiers combed the bush. Many people had life-threatening wounds, he said.[48]

He also said that the Hutu rebels had come from Congo and Rwanda to reinforce their compatriots in Burundi. And Lieutenant-Colonel Sinarunzi said "human losses are very heavy" but still being counted.[49]

The carnage was just one among countless others in a country which has been hobbled by ethnic conflict – in the struggle for power more than anything else – since 1962 when it won independence from Belgium.

The rebels' decision to attack a military base near the capital was undoubtedly intended to achieve maximum impact on the Tutsi military regime and its ethnic supporters by letting them know that they were not safe anywhere in this predominantly Hutu country in spite of

148

the fact that the Hutu majority were powerless.

It may also have stemmed from the fact that the insurgents no longer had much freedom to operate from Congo since Kabila, then Rwanda's and Burundi's and Uganda's ally, became the country's new ruler.

Unlike his predecessor Mobutu Sese Seko who supported the Hutu rebels financially and militarily and allowed them to use Congo (then Zaire) as a launching pad for incursions into Rwanda and Burundi, Kabila was then hostile to the Hutus until he embraced them later as allies in his war against his erstwhile comrades – Rwanda, Burundi, and Uganda – when they invaded his country to try to get rid of him.

But even if the rebels are no longer able to operate from their bases in Congo, they still have the capacity to wreak havoc within Burundi itself, paralyse the government, and extract maximum concessions from any Tutsi-dominated regime by waging a war of attrition indefinitely, sustained by their superiority in numbers as an integral part of the Hutu majority from whom they have always drawn support even though they have alienated some of them with their brutal tactics, especially when they kill fellow Hutus who don't support them as may have been the case with some of the killings on New Year's day in 1998.

As the search for the survivors in the New Year's day attack continued, more casualties were reported. The death toll climbed to 300, including 100 rebels and four government soldiers. And about 7,000 people were displaced when they fled their homes. According to a report from Burundi by Christophe Nkurunziza, a Burundian, in *The Boston Globe*:

"Up to 200 civilians, most of them women and children, died during the assault at Rukaramu settlement and a nearby army camp several miles south of the capital, army spokesman Lieutenant-Colonel Mamert Sinaranzi said....

While international human rights organizations have accused the army of using Hutu civilians as human shields, those aiding yesterday's search (for the attackers) joined voluntarily, said Sinaranzi....

It was unclear whether the civilians were targeted or simply caught in the cross-fire. In other attacks, the rebels...have killed Hutu civilians whom they accuse of denying shelter, money, and recruits to guerrillas....

The army said the Hutu were taking part in yesterday's roundup because they believe they were singled out by the rebels during Thursday's (January 1) attack.

The government's claim was difficult to confirm independently because the army had barred all reporters from the scene except those from state-controlled television, claiming it was too dangerous."[50]

It is doubtful that the survivors joined the search voluntarily, as the army spokesman claimed. Given the army's notorious record of brutality against the Hutu, it is highly probable that any Hutu who did not help the Tutsi army track down the rebels would have been labelled "a rebel" himself, or a rebel sympathiser, and would have risked being shot by Tutsi soldiers.

Another indication that the survivors were coerced into joining the search was the government's decision to bar all reporters from the scene except those working for state-controlled television. If it was dangerous for the other reporters to go to the scene of the massacre, as the government claimed, it was equally dangerous for the state television reporters to go there; and probably even more so, since they worked for the government and would have been prime target for attack by the rebels.

And if the army was able to protect state television reporters, it also could have protected the other reporters as well, had they been allowed to go to the scene of the massacre – as much as it was able to "protect" Hutu civilians who joined the search to help find the attackers.

The state television reporters were allowed to go to the scene of the massacre because, as government employees, they were automatically expected to report favourably on the government and cover up the atrocities committed by the army. As employees of the state-controlled media in a highly repressive state, they could not function as independent reporters but only as megaphones for the Tutsi-dominated regime, echoing what the government wanted to be reported.

But such bias did not change the facts on the ground. The Hutu insurgents were waging a deadly campaign – as were Tutsi soldiers – and continued to do so regardless of how hard the government tried to gloss over the facts, especially regarding its brutal repression of innocent Hutu civilians.

This brutal repression is, only in a more violent way, an extension of the feudal servitude in which the Hutu majority have lived for hundreds of years under the Tutsi. And they will remain at their mercy probably for many years, considering their weakness in spite of their numerical strength:

"Hutus are cynical: though they outnumber the Tutsi six times over, their attempts over the past 30 years to gain power peacefully have been met with murder and repression."[31]

But that is a highly destabilising situation which guarantees only one thing: escalation and perpetuation of the conflict regardless of how many lives the Hutu continue to lose. They still count on their strength in numbers to prevail one day even if it takes 100 years. And they probably will not have to wait that long, may be no more than 30 years.

The New Year's attack which took place shortly before dawn was one of the most daring attempts by the Hutu rebels to strike at the very heart of the Tutsi ethnocracy, the nation's capital Bujumbura and its environs, to demonstrate their commitment to armed struggle as the most effective means to achieve their goal of Hutu emancipation from Tutsi domination, however delusional this may be, right now, considering the country's military might which dwarfs the rebels' capacity to wage war.

But the raid served a psychological purpose of far-reaching consequences. It scared the "invincible" Tutsis. It also dramatised the plight of the Hutu majority which had been largely ignored by the international media except in the case of Rwanda which was highlighted because of the ferocity and magnitude of the 1994 genocide unparalleled in modern history; no other holocaust has claimed so many lives in so short a time, and with so much bloodshed.

The Tutsi – in both Rwanda and Burundi – will never forget that. And any attack by the Hutu rebels reminds them of the fact that there is always a possibility of another holocaust of that magnitude; a fear the Hutu rebels have always exploited by launching more attacks against the Tutsi to create panic throughout the entire community regardless of its unintended consequences, making the Tutsi even more determined to hang on to power out of fear that they will be exterminated if they relinquish control. The New Year's attack was one such raid:

"Shortly before dawn on January 1st, a large group of rebels attacked Burundi's main airport, seizing weapons from the neighbouring garrison. The attack left at least 280 people dead, most of them villagers from nearby Rukaramu.

The army claimed that they had been murdered by the fleeing 'genocidal terrorists.' The rebels say they were killed by the army because of their pro-rebel support. Others say they were caught in crossfire as the soldiers chased the rebels in the darkness.

Most of the bodies seen by independent witnesses had

not been killed by bullets but by blows, many of them from hoes or machetes. That points a finger at the rebels. But...why should they kill their own people?

In Burundi's brutal conflict,...civilians, most of them Hutu, are the pawns and victims. The rebels force their support; the army takes revenge and demands their co-operation.

So all three versions of the new year massacre could be true: rebels killing people who refused to help them, soldiers taking reprisal, some people dying in the confusion....

Both FRODEBU, the main Hutu political party, and the National Council for the Defence of Democracy (CNDD), the Hutu guerrilla force, have grown in strength and militancy.

In December (1997) FRODEBU, which lost power in the coup, acknowledged an exile, Jean Minani, as its leader. And the CNDD rebels have linked up with the (Hutu) former members of the Rwandan army and militia; some of the rebels killed in the airport attack were wearing Rwandan uniforms.

Government claims that the group had fled across the border to Congo proved untrue. The rebels camped a few miles north-west of the capital, Bujumbura, launching another attack on January 6th.

That shows a new confidence: they no longer rely on disruptive hit-and-run tactics. But...the Tutsi-dominated army, which ran the country from 1966 until 1993, shows no sign of negotiating itself out of power."[52]

And the Hutu show no sign of giving up the fight.

The 1998 New Year's raid also set a precedent in terms of stepped-up attacks in and around the capital in this perennial conflict, emboldening the rebels to launch more such invasions in the future. The insurgents launched two more raids in the last week of January, belying the government's claim that the Tutsi military regime had

153

everything under control around the capital after the previous attacks on January 1st and 6th. According to an army spokesman on January 21st, the rebels killed 45 people in two separate attacks in the previous 48 hours. All the victims were civilians except one.

Colonel Isaie Nibizi said the insurgents were members of the National Liberation Front (FNL), the military wing of the Party for the Liberation of the Hutu People (PALIPEHUTU). They killed 32 civilians on January 19th during the night in a settlement in northwest Burundi. He also said 13 people, including one government soldier, were killed in a six-hour attack on January 21st in rural Rumonge commune on the shore of Lake Tanganyika 47 miles south of the capital. But it was not clear which guerrilla group carried out the second attack.[53]

However, what was clear was that the guerrillas had intensified their campaign, mainly to extract concessions from the Tutsi-dominated regime and eventually establish a Hutu-majority government.

Although the Tutsi military rulers did not admit it, the guerrilla war compelled them to take some steps towards a political settlement of the conflict. But one such initiative met with disaster. Burundi's defence minister, Colonel Firmin Sinzoyiheba, was killed on 28 January 1998 when his helicopter crashed in poor weather.

According to Burundian officials, Sinzoyiheba, one of the most powerful figures in the military government, and four others died when the helicopter lost visibility and crashed in the Gihinga Hills, a 6,500-foot-high ridge, about 25 miles southeast of Bujumbura, the capital.

He and his entourage were travelling from Bujumbura to Gitega where the defence minister was to meet with Hutu opposition leaders whose political parties were the umbrella organisations of the armed groups waging guerrilla war against the Tutsi military government.[54] Communications minister, Pierre-Claver Ndayicariye, said there were heavy rains in the area when Colonel

Sinzoyiheba flew in the helicopter on his way to an informal meeting with the Hutu leaders to discuss ways of ending the civil war.[55]

Military head of state Pierre Buyoya also flew to Gitega for the informal peace talks but changed his route to avoid the storm, an indication that no sabotage was involved in the defence minister's helicopter crash.

Sinzoyiheba, a retired colonel, kept a low-profile in the Tutsi-dominated military government but was regarded by diplomats in Bujumbura as being almost as powerful as Buyoya. A Tutsi himself like Buyoya, Sinzoyiheba had also served as defence minister under the ousted president, Sylvestre Ntibantuganya, a Hutu, over whom he exerted enormous influence by virtue of his position as a member of the dominant Tutsi ethnic group and the army.

Tanzanian officials, who had tried but failed to mediate in the civil war, described Sinzoyiheba as a hardliner and the man behind the government's refusal to talk to the rebels.

Therefore it is doubtful that he would have made major concessions, if any, to the Hutu opposition leaders had he attended the meeting in Gitega.

But his decision, as well as Buyoya's, to go to the meeting was an indication that the Tutsi military regime had been forced by the guerrilla fighters to face harsh reality: the government can not win the war, and it can not impose its will on the Hutu majority by military means. It has to win their hearts and minds if there is going to be peace in the country. And that can be achieved only if the Hutu majority are given equal rights and are no longer treated as second-class citizens in their own homeland. The alternative is war which is going to bleed the country to death.

The January 1998 attacks had all the elements for such a prolonged war of attrition. The rebels targeted the capital. They raided a military garrison; launched sustained attacks using heavy weapons; blocked the country's main arteries, and were not neutralised by the army, as demonstrated by their tactical retreat when they camped only a few miles northwest of the capital, waiting for another ambush, and showing no fear of government forces who were so near them. According to *Keesing's Record of World Events*:

"Further rebel attacks on the outskirts of Bujumbura continued throughout January. The main road to the centre and north of the country was temporarily closed on January 11 following skirmishes in its vicinity.

Some 42 rebels were reportedly killed at Isale, 10 kilometres from Bujumbura, on January 14, whilst on January 18 rebels targeted a military post at Gikongo, on the northern outskirts of the capital.

Despite claims by military sources that the rebels had been repulsed, further exchanges of gunfire to the south of Bujumbura were reported on January 22."[56]

The attacks were carried out by more than one group, showing the raids were coordinated. The New Year's attack was carried out by the FDD, the armed wing of the National Council for the Defence of Democracy (CNDD); so were some of the other raids.

The rest were carried out by the National Liberation Front (FNL), the military arm of the Party for the Liberation of the Hutu People (PALIPEHUTU).

The attacks continued the following month. On 12 February 1998, at least 24 civilians were killed and 46 wounded when Hutu rebels attacked a village in southern Burundi, witnesses said. Hundreds of rebels descended from the hills around Minago, 30 miles south of the capital, at night, wielding rifles, machetes, hoes, and hammers and knives, according to a report from Minago. As Athanase Nibizi, a 40-year-old priest who hid inside his church during the three-hour attack, stated: "They killed 24 people. I counted the bodies this morning."[57]

And in the words of 55-year-old Zacharie Kamwenubusa: "Many, many people were killed with machetes, knives, hoes, hammers, and clubs. I saw a young child...hacked in the neck, head, and hand. Many others were killed in the same way."[58]

Witnesses said the dead included men, women, and children. Most were found hacked to death in their own houses. A few hundred yards behind a church and a camp housing several hundred displaced people, Nibizi pointed to 16 fresh graves topped with stick crosses. He said 8 other bodies were buried nearby.

The villagers in Munago said some of the attackers were singing throughout the mayhem, while others fired off rifles and looted property including chickens, goats and beer. "After killing the people, they looted everything. Everybody tried to hide," Kamwenubusa said. A local military commander who did not want to be identified said at least 46 civilians had been injured.[59]

Besides the carnage, it is the increasing level of sophistication and intensity of the attacks which compelled the authorities, especially the Tutsi army, to acknowledge the magnitude of the guerrilla campaign. According to a Reuters report from Minago, Burundi, in *The Boston Globe*:

"A local military commander...said the wounded were evacuated to hospitals in Bujumbura and further south in the lakeside town of Rumonge. Germaine Nteziyorirwa, a female survivor, showed a Reuters correspondent five machete wounds to her head, neck, arm and hands.

Residents and army officers said the rebels had launched an organized assault, striking simultaneously three separate locations around the village....

The military commander...said his soldiers had chased away the attackers, but as he spoke, the sound of automatic gunfire echoed in the distance.

Hutu rebels stepped up their campaign against

Burundi's Tutsi-dominated army and government last month (January 1998), with a New Year's Day offensive on Bujumbura airport and its environs....The fighting has continued in hills around the capital almost everyday since."[60]

The guerrilla campaign was complemented by the economic embargo to try to compel the Tutsi military regime to make substantial concessions to its opponents. On 21 February 1998, the presidents of Tanzania, Rwanda and Uganda, the prime minister of Ethiopia, and the secretary-general of the Organisation of African Unity, unanimously agreed at a meeting in Kampala, Uganda, to maintain regional sanctions against Burundi until the ruling military junta moved towards civilian rule.[61] However, Rwanda's pledge was only symbolic. The Tutsi quasi-military regime in Kigali, Rwanda's capital, did nothing to honour its pledge and, instead, placed ethnic loyalty – support for fellow Tutsis in Burundi – above democratic principles and regional solidarity.

In yet another deadly attack in April 1998, Hutu guerrillas inflicted heavy casualties in their sustained campaign to destabilise the Tutsi government. It was described as the second-most serious offensive since the January 1st attack in which the insurgents captured and briefly occupied Burundi's main airport just outside the capital.

The latest attack took place on 22 April east of Bujumbura. At least 73 people, including 47 rebels, were killed, according to state radio.[62] The rebels attacked Bandagura and Rubingo hills 12 miles east of the capital Bujumbura, killing 26 civilians and wounding at least 10 others. As the state-run radio put it: "Administrative sources say the death toll has risen to 26 civilians dead, and according to the same sources, 47 assailants were killed."[63] They also stole cattle and escaped to the Kibira forest north of Bujumbura.

The attack near the capital, one among several, was also intended to let the government know that the guerrilla force was a factor to be reckoned with. In spite of the military setbacks the rebels suffered, they made it clear that they were still capable of hitting Bujumbura and its surrounding areas with impunity.

Residents of the capital said they heard gunfire to the east of the lakeside city early in the morning; it's on the northeastern shore of Lake Tanganyika.

The rebels were reportedly killed in ensuring clashes with the army. And, as in previous attacks, the insurgents used hoes and machetes during the dawn raid on April 22nd.

The timing of the raid, at dawn, and its location in the vicinity of the capital, had a significant psychological impact on the city's residents including the military rulers who could no longer dismiss lightly the escalation of the offensive.

Military head of state Major Pierre Buyoya continued to pursue a two-track policy of internal reform and attempts to soften or end the economic embargo imposed on his regime. The military junta also continued to wage war against the insurgents of the National Council for the Defence of Democracy (NCDD) and the Party for the Liberation of the Hutu People (PALIPEHUTU). And the two groups, which represented the Hutu majority, continued to push their demands for military reform, democratic elections, and a new constitution while at the same time continuing to wage guerrilla warfare as a leverage or bargaining tool in any negotiations in order to extract maximum concessions from the Tutsi military regime.

But any major concessions by the government would set a precedent, with the Hutu expecting more, as the Tutsi ethnocracy is eroded gradually and eventually collapses; an inconceivable scenario for the Tutsi. It is unthinkable that they would work for their own destruction. That is what democracy means to them in a country where they are vastly outnumbered.

Yet neither side wants to compromise on the basis of a mutually acceptable formula. This is what has prompted some African leaders to concede that the best solution to the Hutu-Tutsi ethnic conflict is separation of the two groups. Each should have its own independent state, as President Daniel arap Moi of Kenya bluntly suggested. According to a report from Nairobi, Kenya, in the *International Herald Tribune*:

"President Daniel arap Moi of Kenya suggested Thursday (9 April 1998) that the Tutsi of Rwanda and Burundi should live in one country and the Hutu in another, the official Kenya News Agency reported. He linked the suggestion to a warning that tribalism could destroy Africa....

Mr. Moi's proposal brought into the open an idea that has long been discussed behind closed doors, but rejected because of the implications it would have for other African countries where boundaries run through tribal groupings, analysts said....'President Moi said that unless Africans were careful, tribalism will destroy the continent completely,' the news agency said."[64]

Tribalism has inflicted enormous damage on both Rwanda and Burundi, with people being killed everyday because of what they are. For instance, on 18 May 1998, 63 people were killed and 12 wounded when armed Hutus attacked camps in two communes in Burundi's northwestern Cibitoke Province.[65] All the victims were Tutsis. This was one of the attacks the Tutsi military regime used to justify its brutal repression of the Hutu majority, targeting all Hutus for the same reason the Hutu rebels attacked the Tutsi in Cibitoke Province: because of what they are.

It is this kind of bigotry which has fuelled the Hutu-

Tutsi ethnic conflict, one of the bloodiest in the history of post-colonial Africa. Attempts to resolve the conflict have achieved nothing through the years.

But despite the deadlock in the quest for peace, further attempts were made to bring the two sides together and try to end the civil war in Burundi. In early May 1998, negotiators said they would try again in June to hold another peace conference.

The peace talks were tentatively scheduled for June 15th in neighbouring Tanzania. A spokesman for the Organisation of African Unity (OAU) said Burundi's Tutsi-dominated government had agreed to attend the meeting after backing out of an earlier round of talks in August 1997, citing bias and security concerns.[66]

The Tutsi have always accused Tanzania of favouring the Hutu. Tanzania and other countries, as well as human rights workers and missionaries who have worked in Burundi through the years, accuse the Tutsi of oppressing the Hutu; a charge the Tutsi military regime seems to have inadvertently conceded when it promulgated a new constitution in June 1998, mainly as a result of intensified guerrilla attacks and economic sanctions imposed on Burundi by its neighbours in August 1996 but enforced especially by Tanzania and Kenya.

On 6 June 1998, President Pierre Buyoya signed into law a transitional constitution which, theoretically, laid the foundation for sweeping changes in the country's Tutsi-dominated government. The constitution replaced the decree Buyoya passed after he came to power in July 1996.

If implemented, the reform measures embodied in the transitional constitution would have marked the first time in almost two years that the Hutu FRODEBU party, ousted from power in the 1996 military coup, would have started having considerable say in the Tutsi-led government. FRODEBU member of parliament Leonidas Ntibayazi said the transitional accord aimed to "restore peace and

161

make equilibrium in all sectors – in the army, in the economy, in the justice system, and socially."[67]

Members of parliament and other officials said the new transitional constitution provided for a range of institutional reforms including replacing the post of prime minister with two vice presidents, enlarging parliament from 81 to 121, and reducing the overall size of government.

But the new constitution was also a major concession to the Tutsi who engineered and executed the 1996 military coup. It combined some elements of Buyoya's 1996 decree – the edict was tailored to suit the interests of the powerful Tutsi who put him power; otherwise he would not have issued it – with the 1992 democratic constitution which was suspended after the coup.

Peace Process Minister Ambroise Niyonsaba said a government reshuffle was likely to begin the same week the new constitution was signed into law, with Buyoya selecting two vice presidents.[68] Members of parliament said the first vice president responsible for political and administrative affairs was likely to come from FRODEBU. To help reduce hostilities, a Hutu would have to fill such a powerful post. That is why the Hutu FREDOBU party was almost guaranteed to get the job.

The transitional constitution was part of a comprehensive peace initiative led by Tanzania's former president, Julius Nyerere.

But at the peace talks in Arusha, Tanzania, in June 1998, delegates of the Tutsi military junta and the rebel representatives were divided over the question of a cease-fire. In what amounted to a concession to the rebels and to the East and Central African leaders, because of the cumulative impact of the guerrilla campaign and the economic embargo, the Tutsi regime's representatives at the peace talks in Tanzania said they wanted a cease-fire but also an end to the sanctions. However, the rebels of the National Council for the Defence of Democracy (CNDD), the largest Hutu opposition group, rejected the cease-fire and linkage of the two.

The peace talks started on 15 June 1998 under the chairmanship of Julius Nyerere. According to a report from Arusha, Tanzania, in *The Boston Globe*:

"The talks brought together the government and the National Council for the Defense of Democracy for the first time under Nyerere, who has not visited Burundi for two years, in part for security reasons.

In the initial stages of the talks, Nyerere, Tanzania's founding president, is seeking common ground on a cease-fire, the future of sanctions, and a commitment to progress to a second round, delegates said....

The Burundi government delegation said after private consultations with Nyerere it was willing to agree to a 'cessation of hostilities' and was committed to the talks.

Nyerere yesterday (17 June 1998) continued private talks (with political leaders and rebels groups).

Diplomats said the National Council for the Defense of Democracy was opposed both to a cease-fire and to the lifting of sanctions.

Nyerere recognizes National Council founder Leonard Nyangoma as the group's legal representative, even though it remains unclear how much influence he holds over its armed wing, the Forces for the Defense of Democracy, one diplomat said. The rebel group is split and one faction protested yesterday its exclusion from the talks."[69]

The refusal by the National Council for the Defence of Democracy to accept a cease-fire and an end to economic sanctions was deeply rooted in their mistrust of the Tutsi military regime. They did not believe it would honour its commitment to the peace process. They also had history on their side – unfulfilled promises, atrocities against the Hutu which were never addressed and whose perpetrators were never punished – all the way since independence in

1962.

It is a tragic history which includes the assassination of Hutu leaders and the extermination of the Hutu elite – to deprive the Hutu of effective leadership – their colleagues at the peace talks in Tanzania never forgot. As *The Economist* stated:

"At one time Burundi's history of ethnic massacres was even more savage than Rwanda"s. So after Rwanda's 1994 genocide, many people assumed that Burundi was on the brink of a similar tragedy....

Out of the 81 members of the 1993 parliament, 23 have been murdered – all of them from the majority, mainly Hutu, FRODEBU party. Many others have fled into exile, some joining militant Hutu movements."[70]

It is these militants – some of whom were moderate before – who took the most uncompromising stand during the peace talks, while some of the most intransigent among them were excluded from the negotiations. On the Tutsi side, there were just as many with an equally inflexible attitude.

The road to peace remained filled with land mines.

Stalemate: Peace without Compromise

In spite of the intransigence of the Tutsi military regime, the peace negotiations in Tanzania were partly facilitated by Pierre Buyoya and his supporters in and outside the government. As soon as Burundi's neighbours imposed economic sanctions on the landlocked nation, Buyoya started working on an agreement with what was left of parliament and its dominant FRODEBU party which won the 1993 elections. It was this agreement which was discussed at the peace talks in Arusha, Tanzania, and which Buyoya hoped would be accepted by

Hutu militants, Burundi's neighbours, and by the chief negotiator, Julius Nyerere.

The agreement was endorsed by FRODEBU members of parliament and their Tutsi counterparts, but after a stormy debate in the National Assembly on 4 June 1998. And it was on the basis of this accord that Buyoya had himself formally sworn as president of Burundi, ending his status as a *de facto* head of state.

The new law – transitional constitution – allowed for the creation of a coalition government comprising 22 cabinet members, 11 of whom would come from the opposition; the replacement of the prime minister by two vice presidents, one Hutu and the other Tutsi; and the enlargement of the national legislature, as we learned earlier.

But this constitutionally mandated power-sharing agreement was vehemently denounced by militants on both sides. The chairman of the Tutsi UPRONA party who was also one of the most uncompromising Tutsi hardliners, Charles Mukasi, still refused to talk to the *genocidaires* (as he called them) of the main Hutu FRODEBU party, and did not go to Arusha, Tanzania, for the peace talks. But his party, which supported Buyoya's peace initiative, sent representatives and backed the proposed power-sharing agreement.

On the Hutu side, FRODEBU was also splintered, but the main group supported the peace process. However, the major militant group, the National Council for the Defence of Democracy (CNDD) denounced the agreement as "an act of treason" and vowed it will continue waging guerrilla warfare.

Yet, even the CNDD itself was divided, and its founder Leonard Nyangoma, who led one of the factions, went to Arusha for the peace talks and met Buyoya face-to-face. And two other militant Hutu groups also sent delegates to the peace conference. But given the intractable nature of the problem, prospects for conflict resolution in Burundi remained bleak at best.

The warring parties signed a cease-fire agreement in Arusha, Tanzania, on 21 June 1998. But the agreement was violated by both sides. In fact, it was hardly enforced. According to reports from Burundi, about 13,000 people fled renewed clashes between Hutu guerrillas and Tutsi government soldiers in the northern part of the country in the last week of July 1998. President Buyoya conceded that the cease-fire existed only on paper and questioned whether rebel leader Leonard Nyangoma controlled his forces.[71]

Fighting continued throughout the year and, in a rare admission, the government acknowledged its own excesses against civilians. Saying "there were errors and we have to come clean about it," a government spokesman admitted that army troops had killed "around 30" innocent civilians in a clash with Hutu rebels on 3 – 4 November 1998. But he denied reports that 178 civilians had died at Mutambu, 22 miles southeast of the capital.

Although he admitted wrongdoing, this was the only second time that the Tutsi-dominated government had acknowledged responsibility for killing Hutu civilians,[72] whom it has always targeted for reprisals, in retaliation for attacks by the rebels – even if they don't support them. And there was evidence showing that Tutsi soldiers had killed more civilians than the government was willing to admit. According to *Keesing's Record of World Events*:

"Amid continued reports of killings during the month (of November 1998), the Agence France-Press (AFP) news agency reported on November 10 that at least 100 Hutu civilians had been massacred by soldiers of the Tutsi-dominated army at Mutambu, near the capital Bujumbura, in early November.

The killings were said to have been carried out in retaliation for an earlier attack on a camp which was sheltering Tutsis, by fighters of the National Liberation

166

Forces (FNL), the armed wing of the Hutu-based PALIPEHUTU movement.

On November 14 government officials said three army officers had been arrested in connection with a massacre of 30 civilians at Mutambu, an incident which was described as a botched operation against Hutu rebels.

Severin Ntahomvukiye, the External Relations and Co-operation Minister, said on November 3 that there had been an attempt to form a new group. He did not identify the group but confirmed that a number of people had been arrested."[73]

Then two months later in January 1999, the leaders of the seven African countries which imposed economic sanctions on Burundi agreed to suspend them, pending more progress in ending the civil war.[74] The embargo was really being enforced by Tanzania, more than any other country, because of her strategic position as conduit for Burundi's imports and exports and her determination to help resolve the Hutu-Tutsi conflict.

The decision to suspend sanctions was one of several steps the East African heads of state took at their meeting in Arusha, Tanzania, aimed at increasing cooperation among the countries in the region. The talks specifically sought to achieve integration of Rwanda and Burundi into the East African bloc which was working towards regional solidarity in several areas.

Rwanda and Burundi have really never been an integral part of the East African community of nations, which is mostly Anglophone, because of their civil conflicts and especially their ties to the Francophone bloc. As former Belgian colonies, they have historical ties to Francophone countries and use French as their official language, unlike the rest of the East African countries – Kenya, Uganda and Tanzania – which use English.

Although the economic embargo imposed on Burundi was intended to be a punitive measure, it also drew the country into the orbit as an integral part of the East African bloc. Unfortunately, no significant progress towards ending the civil war – which was the main condition for suspending economic sanctions – was made in the following months to justify continued suspension of the embargo.

In spite of the mutual suspicion between the main parties to the conflict, the parties involved concluded another round of peace talks in Tanzania towards the end of March 1999 and reported "some progress."[75]

The peace process was facilitated in another way when two months later the Tutsi soldiers who assassinated Burundi's first Hutu president, Melchior Ndadaye in October 1993, were convicted of the murder. On 14 May 1999, the Supreme Court of Burundi sentenced five soldiers to death for the assassination. The court convicted 39 people and acquitted 38 in the assassination trial. The Justice Ministry said prison terms handed down ranged from one year to 20 years.[76]

It was this assassination as part of an attempted coup by Tutsi soldiers, just four months after Ndadaye assumed office, which plunged the country into chaos, triggering a wave of massacres and a civil war between the Tutsi-dominated army and the Hutu rebels.

Those sentenced to death were Lieutenant Paul Kamana, in exile in Uganda; Laurence Nzeyimana; Juvénal Gahungu; Sylvere Nduwumukama; and Emmanuel Ndayizeye.[77] They were responsible for one of the most gruesome political murders on the African continent in which President Ndadaye was bayoneted to death.

All the accused, who were Tutsi, pleaded not guilty.[78] Yet the evidence against them was overwhelming, more than enough to justify the sentences imposed on them.

Unfortunately, the real culprits behind the assassination were left untouched because they were powerful individuals in the army and in the country as a whole. And they were all Tutsi like the killers themselves.

Although Ndadaye's assassins were brought to justice, their conviction did not improve relations or bridge the ethnic divide between the Hutu and the Tutsi; nor was it expected to, despite its powerful symbolism as a conciliatory gesture. It was, undoubtedly, hailed by some Hutus as a triumph of justice in this particular case. Yet a comprehensive peace agreement – mandating dispensation of justice across the spectrum for all Hutus, and no less for the Tutsi – would require more than just a few cases of restorative and retributive justice.

The peace process was virtually derailed by the continuation of clashes between the Hutu rebels and the Tutsi army during the following months in what was apparently an escalation of hostilities by both sides to achieve maximum political and military advantages they could use as a bargaining tool in future negotiations. Both sides were losers. There was no winner without peace.

Some of the biggest conflicts took place in August 1999 when Hutu insurgents and Tutsi soldiers clashed outside the capital Bujumbura. Thousands of civilians fled the surrounding areas and sought refuge in the capital.[79] And villagers accused the Tutsi-dominated army of killing 147 Hutu civilians in revenge for a Hutu rebel attack that took place on August 10th. But a Defence Ministry spokesman blamed the rebels for the killings, despite evidence to the contrary and eyewitness accounts by some of the victims who survived the mayhem.[80]

One of the biggest rebel attacks took place on 29 August 1999. It lasted from midnight to dawn, resulting in at least 46 deaths. The offensive, which rocked the capital and terrified tens of thousands of its residents, targeted parts of Bujumbura inhabited by Tutsis – as almost the entire city was, after the ethnic cleansing of the Hutu following the 1996 Tutsi-engineered military coup in which President Sylvestre Ntibantunganya, a Hutu, was ousted.

169

The August attack came at a critical time as a new round of negotiations – seen as crucial if the country's fragile peace process were to take hold – drew near in Arusha, Tanzania,[81] and was obviously calculated to disrupt the peace initiative. The attack not only rocked the capital but also spread fear of escalating violence across the country between the Hutu and the Tutsi, and was a major blow to the peace process.[82]

Nyerere Dies

The peace process suffered another major setback within two months of the Hutu offensive when Julius Nyerere, Tanzania's first president and chief mediator in Burundi's conflict, died of leukaemia on 14 October 1999 in a hospital in London, England. He was 77.

His role as a mediator in African conflicts was widely acknowledged. And in the case of Burundi, no other negotiator had Nyerere's stature or could command as much respect as he did from both sides to the conflict.

A scholarly statesman and consummate politician, he was confident of himself in academic circles as much as he was at ease among peasants because of his ascetic lifestyle and genuine commitment to equality and justice for all, from the most humble to the most exalted. He left a void that will be difficult to fill. As *The Economist* stated:

"Although his socialist policies were criticised, his integrity and erudition were much admired....A deeply principled man, Julius Nyerere was that rare – and not always fortunate – sort of idealist who had a chance to put his ideals into practice....He was a preacher as much as a politician....

No one questioned his sincerity, and his integrity was widely admired. Unlike many African leaders of his generation he lived simply and was not corrupt.

He gave Tanzania stability and unity. Under his one-party rule it was politically peaceful and it was spared civil war....

Though honest himself, his moral example was not enough to prevent the widespread theft of foreign aid. A believer in justice, he...(was) as keen on equality as on economic growth....

Compared to some of his neighbours, Mr. Nyerere was an angel....Although late in life Mr. Nyerere did acknowledge that his socialist experiments had failed, his idealism never left him. In retirement, he even tried to reform the ruling party. Finding it inert and ineradicably corrupt, he changed his mind about one-party rule.

Admirers will say that Julius Nyerere was too idealistic for this world and that bad implementation does not negate his dream of equality. To critics, his moral approach to politics masked an arrogance and a refusal to listen to those with shrewder views of what was best for his country.

Tanzanians abandoned ujamaa (familyhood, African socialism) as soon as they could. Yet Mr. Nyerere himself remained extraordinarily popular. His policies had failed, but people admired his sincerity and his ascetic life. His warm and engaging style – in conversation and from a platform – was irresistible....

He bore the title mwalimu or teacher....He was a magnificent teacher: articulate, questioning, stimulating, caring."[83]

And as *Newsweek* put it:

"(Julius Nyerere)...died an international hero....Nyerere's personality was irresistible. Absolute power never corrupted him: he earned $8,000 during his best year. His chosen honorific was Mwalimu – teacher. And under his direction Tanzania's literacy level rose sharply. When Nyerere, 77, died of leukemia last week, the world lost a man of principle."[84]

On a continent no longer under colonial rule but wracked by civil wars, his enormous contribution to the liberation struggle will always be remembered, as much as will his role as a peacemaker and staunch advocate of African unity, for which he will be sorely missed. In the words of *The Christian Science Monitor*:

"His goal of ending white minority rule in Africa, inspired numerous other liberation movements....In retirement, he mediated numerous political crises on the continent."[85]

One of his biggest achievements – besides spearheading the struggle to end white minority rule in Africa probably more than any of his contemporaries besides a few other leaders such as Kwame Nkrumah, Sekou Toure, Modibo Keita, Kenneth Kaunda, and Milton Obote – was the creation and consolidation of Tanzania as a union of two independent states (Tanganyika and Zanzibar), the only such union on the entire continent.

He left behind a stable and peaceful country, a rare phenomenon on this highly unstable and embattled continent. As Keith Richburg, the *Washington Post* Africa bureau chief during the 1990s, states in his book, *Out of America: A Black Man Confronts Africa*:

"One of my earliest trips was to Tanzania, and there I found a country that had actually managed to purge itself of the evil of tribalism.

Under Julius Nyerere and his ruling socialists, the government was able to imbue a true sense of nationalism that transcended the country's natural ethnic divisions, among other things by vigorous campaigns to upgrade education and to make Swahili a truly national language....Tanzania is one place that has succeeded in removing the linguistic barrier that separates so many of Africa's warring factions.

But after three years traveling the continent, I've found that Tanzania is the exception, not the rule. In Africa,...it *is* all about tribes.

Tribalism is what prompted tens of thousands of Rwandan Hutus to pick up machetes and hoes and panga knives and farming tools to bash in the skulls and sever the limbs of their Tutsi neighbors. Tribalism is why entire swaths of Kenya's scenic Rift Valley lie in scorched ruins, why Zulu gunmen in ski masks mow down Xhosa workers outside a factory gate in South Africa, and why thousands of hungry displaced Kasai huddle under plastic sheeting at a remote train station in eastern Zaire (thousands were massacred, disemboweled, and mutilated in Shaba – formerly Katanga – Province, in 1993). And it is tribalism under another name – clans, subclans, factions – that caused young men in Mogadishu to shell the city to oblivion and loot what was left of the rubble."[86]

And as Philip Ochieng', a prominent Kenyan journalist and political analyst who worked at the *Daily News* in Dar es Salaam, Tanzania, in the early 1970s when I was a news reporter of the same paper, stated in his article, "Mwalimu Nyerere's Bequest to Mkapa a Tall Order," in *The Nation*, Nairobi, Kenya, 16 October 1999, two days after Nyerere died:

"Nyerere...never appointed any official or allowed one to be appointed on any other basis than qualification, inclination and experience. This contributed a great deal to making Tanzania the most united country in Africa.

This unity and sharp national consciousness was contributed to by two other life-works of the Teacher (Mwalimu Nyerere). One was that he insisted on uniform Kiswahili throughout the Republic. During the three years that I worked in Dar es Salaam I rarely heard any tribal language being spoken.

The other was what Mwalimu called *Elimu yenye manufaa*. This 'functional education' was much more than what we in Kenya call *elimu ya ngumbaru* ('adult education'). Though beneficiaries specialised in a technique, education was always holistic. As a result, 'poor' Tanzania has one of the highest literacy rates (almost 100) in the world, many times above that of Kenya."

Ten years after Nyerere died, Ochieng' also wrote the following about the late Tanzanian leader in his article, "Africa's Greatest Leader Was A Heroic Failure," *The East African*, Nairobi, 19 October 2009:

"Julius Nyerere is among the extremely few world leaders who have selflessly attempted great things for their national peoples.

Other African leaders — notably Leopold Senghor and Tom Mboya — have spoken of "African socialism" as a means of restoring human dignity to the African person after a protracted era of colonial brutalisation and dehumanisation. But none has ever offered a plausible definition of 'African socialism.'

Mwalimu Nyerere was the first – probably the only – African nationalist leader to cast a serious moral and intellectual eye upon Africa's "extended family" tradition and weave a practical national development philosophy around it.

Ujamaa had two basic components.

The Ujamaa Village was an attempt to revive traditional rural communalism – bringing groups of villages together, investing collectively in them and running them through modern democratic precepts.

Since the turn of the 21st century, Kenya's own leaders have divided and sub-divided what used to be called districts into veritable village units, claiming a purpose similar to 'Nyerereism' – to bring utilities and social services 'closer to the people.'

The second component was much more theoretically shaky – a series of nationalisations intended to bring urban commerce and industry under state control, the state purporting to be the public's trustee.

But the 1967 Arusha Declaration in which this doctrine of "socialism and self-reliance" was enunciated opened a Pandora's box of ideology. Ideas ran from the extreme right to others that were so leftist that, in the circular prism of ideas, they actually bordered on the right!

In a single-party system, all these ideas were forced to contend with one another within that party.

It was no wonder, then, that Marxist-Leninists, Bepari (capitalists) and even Kabaila (feudalists) held central positions both in the party and in government.

This, indeed, was where Nyerere began to reveal his greatness.

In other 'socialist' situations – such as Sekou Toure's Conakry – every thought and activity deemed dangerous would simply have been banned, often on pain of death. Nyerere encouraged even his bitterest opponents to express themselves freely and without fear.

And he often took them on – not by means of such state machinery as our Nyayo House basement, but intellectually, replying to each critic point by point.

The Nationalist (the party's own organ) and *The Standard* Tanzania (the government publication on which Ben Mkapa and I worked – later renamed Daily News) routinely published news, features, columns and letters expressing the most diverse views.

Nyerere demanded only that his detractors produce the facts and figures and weave these into cogent thought.

'Argue, don't shout!' he once admonished his equivalents of the loudmouthed but empty-headed coalition that rules Kenya....

By replacing the colonial educational structure with what he called Elimu yenye Manufaa ('functional education'), he enabled Tanzania to kill up to five birds with one stone.

Tanzanian is the only African country that has totally banished illiteracy, and the Three Rs are solidly linked to vocational interests.

In the process, Tanzania became the African country with the highest degree of national self-consciousness and – through it and through Kiswahili – has almost annihilated the bane of Kenya that we call tribalism....

Any nation that tries to cultivate self-sufficiency, self-efficiency, self-respect and self-pride will find it morally compelling to share these ideals with other nations the world over.

Ujamaa inspired Tanzania into spending much of its meagre resources on liberating the rest of Africa and the world from the colonial yoke.

At a time when Nairobi was drowning in crude elite grabbing, Dar es Salaam was a Mecca of the world's national liberation movements, and a hotbed of global intellectual thought.

From this perspective, it is justifiable to say that Mwalimu Julius Kambarage, son of Chief Nyerere, is the greatest and most successful leader that Africa has ever produced since the European colonial regime collapsed 50 years ago."

Unfortunately, Tanzania's success in combating tribalism and other vices under the leadership of Nyerere has not been emulated by others in the region. In fact, tribalism threatens to destroy Kenya, and even Uganda. And it has almost destroyed other African countries.

It is tribalism which almost destroyed Nigeria during the sixties when the Igbos of the Eastern Province seceded from the federation after tens of thousands of their kinsmen – at least 30,000 – were massacred in the North by the Hausa-Fulani.

Tanzania under Nyerere was the first country to

recognise Biafra (Eastern Nigeria) as an independent state on moral grounds as a protest against the massacre of the Igbos – as well as other Easterners – and the unwillingness of the Federal and Northern Nigerian authorities to protect the victims. As Nyerere stated:

"Unity can only be based on the general consent of the people involved. The people must feel that this state, or this nation, is theirs; and they must be willing to have their quarrels in that context. Once a large number of the people of any such political unit stop believing that the state is theirs, and that the government is their instrument, then the unit is no longer viable. It will not receive the loyalty of its citizens.

For the citizen's duty to serve, and if necessary to die for, his country stems from the fact that it is his and that its government is the instrument of himself and his fellow citizens. The duty stems, in other words, from the common denominator of accepted statehood, and from the state government's responsibility to protect all the citizens and serve them all. For, states, and governments, exist for men and for the service of man. They exist for the citizens' protection, their welfare, and the future well-being of their children. There is no other justification for states and governments except man.

In Nigeria this consciousness of a common citizenship was destroyed by the events of 1966, and in particular by the pogroms in which 30,000 Eastern Nigerians were murdered, many more injured, and about two million forced to flee from the North of their country. It is these pogroms, and the apparent inability or unwillingness of the authorities to protect the victims, which underlies the Easterners' conviction that they have been rejected by other Nigerians and abandoned by the Federal Government.

Whether the Easterners are correct in their belief that they have been rejected is a matter for argument. But they do have this belief. And if they are wrong, they have to be convinced that they are wrong. They will not convinced by being shot. Nor will their acceptance as part of the Federation be demonstrated by the use of Federal power to bomb schools and hospitals in the areas to which people have fled from persecution."[87]

There are striking similarities between Nigeria and Burundi – as well as Rwanda – with regard to massacres perpetrated along ethnic lines, while the authorities do nothing to stop the killings. Sometimes they encourage and even help the killers.

It is these pogroms and other atrocities committed by the Tutsi-dominated army against the Hutu in Burundi – and in neighbouring Rwanda – which threaten to destroy the country as a single political entity; a tragedy Tanzania – although a country of 126 tribes – was able to avoid under the astute leadership of President Nyerere. As *The Christian Science Monitor* stated:

"Tanzania is the only country in sub-Saharan Africa, which, thanks to the nationalist policies of Julius Nyerere...forged a sense of national identity strong enough to eclipse tribal affiliation."[88]

Nyerere was eulogised beyond Africa. *The New York Times* hailed his achievements and described him as "an uncharacteristically humble and modest national leader...idealistic, principled." It went on to state:

"Julius K. Nyerere, the founding father of Tanzania,...used East Africa as a pulpit from which to spread his socialist philosophy worldwide....

Mr. Nyerere became one of the most prominent of the first generation of politicians to head newly independent African states as colonialism ebbed, playing a leading role in the debate over economic inequalities between the

Northern and Southern Hemispheres.

When he guided what had been the British Trust Territory of Tanganyika into sovereignty in 1961, he was the youngest of the continent's triumphant nationalists, a group that included Kwame Nkrumah of Ghana, Jomo Kenyatta of Kenya, Kenneth Kaunda of Zambia and Felix Houphouet-Boigny of Ivory Coast.

When he stepped down as President 24 years later, he was only the third modern African leader to relinquish power voluntarily on a continent that by then included 50 independent states ((the other two leaders were Ahmadou Ahidjo of Cameroon and Leopold Sedar Senghor of Senegal). He went neither to jail nor into exile, but to a farm in Butiama, his home village, near the shore of Lake Victoria....

After a vast investment in education, literacy rose phenomenally, and 83 percent of Tanzanians were able to read and write. Mr. Nyerere also succeeded in promoting Swahili so that it superseded dozens of tribal tongues to become a true national language....

The debate over Mr. Nyerere's leadership extended beyond his tenure, with academics, politicians and development strategists often dividing sharply over his legacy.

His domestic and international defenders, generally people of the left, praised his emphasis on social investments and his egalitarian economic policies, crediting them with creating a culturally cohesive nation that avoided ethnic conflict while life expectancy, literacy and access to water increased.

His Tanzanian supporters took pride in Mr. Nyerere's reputation as one of the most prominent proponents of a new economic order that would benefit the developing South in economic relations with the industrial North.

Mr. Nyerere also gained international prestige for his principled support of the struggles for majority rule in South Africa, Namibia, Zimbabwe, Mozambique and

Angola, and for Tanzania's military counter-offensive against Idi Amin of Uganda, which routed the dictator and sent him into exile.

The Third World honored him, and he won the respect of such Western leaders as Olof Palme, Pierre Trudeau, Willy Brandt and Jimmy Carter.

Still, his critics, who included free-market liberals and conservatives, condemned him for adopting paternalistic and coercive policies like ujamaa....

By the time Mr. Nyerere gave up the last vestiges of political power, when he retired as chairman of the single political party,...almost 70 percent of the people had been prodded to move from traditional lands into paternalistically planned villages – ujamaa – in what became Africa's largest and most debated example of social engineering....

His critics...deplored his insistence on one-party rule and price controls, which they said stultified Tanzania's economy, shrank agricultural production, encouraged corruption and led to vast squandering of foreign aid....

The distance Mr. Nyerere traveled from his birth to political power and to the center of an international polemic on development was enormous, spanning ages as well as years....

He was spotted as an exceedingly bright child by the White Fathers, the priests who ran the (boarding) school, and in 1936 he placed first in the entire territory (of Tanganyika) on an entrance exam for a school in Tabora...which was patterned on private schools in Britain....

He went to Makerere University in Uganda, and...won a scholarship to Edinburgh University, where he earned a master's degree in history and economics....

Mr. Nyerere became the Third World's most assertive exponent of the new economic order in which the economic imbalance between the North and South would be overcome through international law and obligation rather than through markets or charity....

Mr. Nyerere reinforced his reputation abroad by his steadfast support of liberation movements....He provided training camps for the African National Congress from South Africa and...support for national movements fighting in Mozambique and Rhodesia (as well as in Angola and Namibia).

And in 1978, after Uganda annexed a 710-square-mile section of Tanzania, Mr. Nyerere angrily denounced Idi Amin, the Ugandan despot,...(and) with startling bluntness, he added:

'There is this tendency in Africa to think that it does not matter if an African kills other Africans. Had Amin been white, free Africa would have passed many resolutions condemning him. Being black is becoming a certificate to kill fellow Africans'....

After he retired, Mr. Nyerere was often asked whether he had any regrets. In a typical interview, he said he was pleased that 'Tanzanians have more sense of national identity than many other Africans,' and he expressed pride in the nation's high rate of literacy....

'What would I have changed if I had my time again? Not much.'

The white-haired farmer, the Mwalimu, then turned to his attempts to instill his idea of African socialism.

'They keep saying you've failed,' he mused. 'But what is wrong with urging people to pull together? Did Christianity fail because the world isn't all Christian?'"[89]

A true Pan-Africanist, Nyerere died while still in the process of trying to help neighbouring Burundi forge a genuine sense of national identity on the anvil of African brotherhood in one of the most terror-ridden countries on the continent;[90] a country torn by ethnic conflict between the Hutu and the Tutsi – people who are so close, yet so far apart simply because they don't belong to the same "tribe"; although it's hard to find tribes which speak the same language, have the same culture, and the same history for hundreds of years like the Hutu and the Tutsi do.

Prospects for peace in Burundi remained bleak, as the world entered another millennium.

Many Hutu militants remained opposed to peace negotiations; so were Tutsi hardliners. And any settlement that excludes them only spells disaster for Burundi.

Hutu militants – as well as Tutsi hardliners – must be part of the solution. Their concerns, fears and aspirations must be taken into account. Otherwise they will always be a major problem.

As members of the largest ethnic group from which they can draw support because their people are oppressed by the Tutsi minority, Hutu militants have the capacity to wreak havoc across this troubled land for decades. The same fate awaits Rwanda.

Notes

Part One

1. Leon Mugesira, quoted by Michael Chege, "Africa's Murderous Professors," in *The National Interest*, No. 46, Washington, D.C., Winter 1996/97, p. 34.

2. Hassan Ngeze, editor of *Kangura*, a Hutu newspaper, Gisenyi, Rwanda, ibid.

3. *La Medaille*, Kigali, Rwanda, February 1994, ibid.

4. Michael Chege, Ibid. See also Emmanuel Bugingo, quoted by Robert Block, "Labour of Love at a School of Hate," in *The Independent*, London, 8 January 1995; *Rwanda: Massive and Systematic Violation of Human Rights from October 1990*, Paris: International Human Rights Foundation, 1993; Gérard Prunier, *The Rwanda Crisis: History of A Genocide* (New York: Columbia University Press, 1997); Philip Gourevitch, *We Wish to Inform You That Tomorrow We Will Be Killed with Our*

Families: Stories from Rwanda (New York: Farrar, Straus & Giroux, 1998); Rosamond Halsey Carr with Ann Howard Halsey, *Land of A Thousand Hills: My Life in Rwanda* (New York: Viking, 1999).

5. René Lemarchand, "The Fire in the Great Lakes," in *Current History: A Journal of Contemporary World Affairs*, May 1999, p. 196. See also R. Lemarchand, *Burundi: Ethnic Conflict and Genocide* (New York: Cambridge University Press, 1996).

6. Philip Gourevitch, "The Psychology of Slaughter: In Uganda, An Echo of the Rwandan Horror," in *The New York Times*, Op-Ed Sunday, 7 March 1999, p. WK-15. See also P. Gourevitch, *We Wish to Inform You That Tomorrow We Will Be Killed with Our Families: Stories from Rwanda*, op. cit.

7. R. Lemarchand, "The Fire in the Great Lakes," op. cit., p. 198. See also George B. N. Ayittey, Africa in Chaos (New York: St. Martin's Press, 1998), pp. 54 – 57.

8. R. Lemarchand, ibid., p. 197.

9. *Rwanda in Reader's Digest Almanac and Yearbook: 1986* (Pleasantville, New York: Reader's Digest Association, Inc., 1985), p. 639.

10. Vincent Gasana and Alfred Ndahiro, "Zaire Crisis Provokes Cry of Tribalism," in *Africa Analysis: The Fortnightly Bulletin on Financial and Political Trends*, No. 259, London, 1 November 1996, p. 15. See also *Broadcasting Genocide – Censorship, Propaganda and State-Sponsored Violence in Rwanda 1990 – 1994* (London: Article 19, 33 Islington High Street, 1996).

11. Godfrey Mwakikagile, Chapter Three: Ethnic Cleansing in Rwanda and Burundi: In Search of An Alternative to The Modern African State, *The Modern African State: Quest for Transformation* (Huntington, New York: Nova Science Publishers, 2001), pp. 73 – 107; G. Mwakikagile, *Africa After Independence: Realities of Nationhood* (Dar es Salaam, Tanzania: New Africa Press, 2009); Colin Legum and john Drysdale, eds., Africa

Contemporary Record: Annual Survey and Documents 1968 – 1969 (London: Africa Research Ltd., 1969), p. 442. See also Jorge G. Castañeda, *Compañero: The Life and Death of Che Guevara* (New York: Alfred A. Knopf, 1997), pp. 276 – 325, 326 – 338, 346 – 347, 356, 367, and 386; Madeleine G. Kalb, *The Congo Cables: The Cold War in Africa – From Eisenhower to Kennedy* (New York: Macmillan, 1982); David Gibbs, *The Political Economy of Third World Intervention: Mines, Money and U.S. Policy in the Congo* (Chicago: University of Chicago Press, 1991).

12. Crawford Young, "Zaire: The Unending Crisis," in *Foreign Affairs*, Fall 1978, p. 178. See also C. Young, *Politics in the Congo* (Madison: University of Wisconsin Press, 1978); Otto Klineberg and Merisa Zavalloni, *Nationalism and Tribalism Among African Students* (Paris: Mouton, 1969).

13. Che Guevara, quoted by R. Lemarchand, "The Fire in the Great Lakes," op. cit., p. 199. See also Che's diary on the Congo, Ernesto Che Guevara, *Pasajes de la guerra revolucionaira* (el Congo), 1966; Rolando E. Bonachea and Nelson P. Valdes, eds., *Che: Selected Works of Ernesto Guevara* (Cambridge: Massachusetts, MIT Press, 1969).

14. Che Guevara, *Pasajes de la guerra revolucionaira* (el Congo), quoted by J. G. Castañeda, *Compañero: The Life and Death of Che Guevara*, op. cit., p. 164. See also G. Michael Schartberg, *Mobutu or Chaos? The United States and Zaire: 1960 – 1990* (New York and Philadelphia: University Press of America/ Foreign Policy Research Institute, 1991); G. Madelaine Kalb, The Congo Cables (New York: Macmillan, 1982).

15. Gérard Prunier, "The Great Lakes Crisis," in *Current History: A Journal of Contemporary World Affairs*, May 1997, p. 195. See also G. Prunier, *The Rwanda Crisis: History of A Genocide* (New York: Columbia University Press, 1997).

16. "Zaire Rebels Aim to Oust Mobutu," in *Africa Analysis*, op cit., p. 1.

17. Paul Kagame, cited in *The Washington Post*, 9 July 1997, p. A-1.

18. Ehud Barak, quoted by Amos Elon, "Exile's Return," a review of Edward W. Said, *Out of Place: A Memoir* (New York: Alfred A. Knopf, 1999), in *The New York Review of Books*, 18 November 1999, p. 12. Se also Edward W. Said, "The One-State Solution," in *The New York Times Magazine*, 10 January 1999.

19. Paul Kagame, quoted in The Washington Post, op. cit., p. A-18. See also Marina Ottaway, "Africa's 'New Leaders': African Solution or African Pproblem?," in *Current History: A Journal of Contemporary World Affairs*, May 1998, pp. 209 – 213.

20. Godfrey Mwakikagile, *The Modern African State: Quest for Transformation*, op. cit.; George B.N. Ayittey, *Africa in Chaos* (New York: St. Martin's Press, 1998); G.B.N. Ayittey, *Africa Betrayed* (New York: St. Martin's Press, 1992); Seyoum Y. Hameso, *Ethnicity and Nationalism in Africa* (Commack, New York: Nova Science Publishers, Inc., 1997); Wole Soyinka, *The Open Sore of a Continent: A Personal Narrative of the Nigerian Crisis* (New York: Oxford University Press, 1996); Fergal Keane, *Season of Blood: A Rwandan Journey* (New York: Viking, 1996); Chinua Achebe, *The Trouble with Nigeria* (Enugu, Nigeria: Fourth Dimension Publishing, 1985).

Mahmood Mamdani, *Imperialism and Fascism in Uganda* (Lawrenceville, New Jersey: Africa World Press, 1984); David Lamb, *The Africans*, (New York: Random House, 1982); Samuel Decalo, *Coups and Army Rule in Africa: Studies in Military Style* (New Haven, Connecticut: Yale University Press, 1976); W.F. Gutteridge, *Military Regimes in Africa* (London: Methuen, 1975); Anton Bebler, ed., *Military Rule in Africa: Dahomey, Ghana, Sierra Leone, and Mali* (1973); Jeffrey T. Strate, *Post-Military Coup Strategy in Uganda: Amin's*

Early Attempts to Consolidate Political Support in Africa (1973); Henry Kyemba, A State of Blood (1973); Godfrey Mwakikagile, *Military Coups in West Africa Since The Sixties* (Huntington, New York: Nova Science Publishers, Inc., 2001).

René Lemarchand, *Burundi: Ethnocide as Discourse and Practice* (Cambridge: Cambridge University Press, 1994); Gebru Takeke, *Ethiopia: Power and Protest* (1991); Amii Olara-Otunnu, *Politics and The Military in Uganda: 1890 – 1985* (1987); Robert A. Dibie, *The Military-Bureaucracy Relationship in Nigeria: Public Policy and Implementation* (Westport, Connecticut: Praeger Publishers, 1999); Larry Diamond, Anthony Kirk-Greene, and Oyeleye Oyediran, *Transition Without End: Nigerian Politics and Civil Society under Babangida* (Boulder, Colorado: Lynne Rienner, 1997); Howard Adelman and Astri Suhrke, ed., *The Path of A Genocide: The Rwanda Crisis fro Uganda to Zaire* (Piscataway, New Jersey: Transaction, 1999).

Ken C. Kotecha and Robert W. Adams, *The Corruption of Power: African Politics* (Washington, D.C.: University Press of America, 1981); Victor LeVine, *Political Corruption: The Ghana Case* (Stanford, California: Hoover Institution Press, 1975); Jean-Francois Bayart, *The State in Africa: The Politics of the Belly* (London: Longman, 1984); Richard Sandbrook, *The Politics of Africa's Stagnation* (New York: Cambridge University Press, 1993); David Waller, *Rwanda: Which Way Now?* (Oxford: Oxfam, 1993); G. E. Boley, *Liberia: The Rise and Fall of the First Republic* (New York: St. Martin's Press, 1983); Peter Anyang' Nyong'o, ed., *Popular Struggles for Democracy in Africa* (London: Zed Books, 1987); Robert E. Jackson and Carl G. Rosberg, *Personal Rule in Black Africa: Prince, Autocrat, Prophet, Tyrant* (Berkeley: University of California Press, 1982).

Nelson Kasfir, *The Shrinking Political Arena: Participation and Ethnicity in African Politics, with a*

Case Study of Uganda (Berkeley: University of California Press, 1976); Crawford Young and Thomas Turner, *The Rise and Decline of the Zairian State* (Madison: University of Wisconsin Press, 1985); Jean-Francois Bayart, Stephen Ellis, and Beatrice Hibou, *The Criminalisation of the State in Africa* (Bloomington: Indiana University Press, 1999); Ngugi wa Thiong'o, *Barrel of Pen: Resistance to Repression in Neo-Colonial Kenya* (Lawrenceville, New Jersey: Africa World Press, 1983); Thomas P. Ofcansky, *Uganda: Tarnished Pearl of Africa* (Boulder, Colorado: Westview Press, 1995); Viva Ona Bartkus, *The Dynamics of Secession: An Analytical Framework* (New York: Cambridge University Press, 1999).

Part Two

1. Burundi, Colin Legum and John Drysdale, eds., *Africa Contemporary Record: Annual Survey and Documents 1968 – 1969* (London: Africa Research Ltd., 1969, p. 141.

2. Ibid., p. 142.

3. Ntare V in *Information Please Almanac: 1998* (Boston: Houghton Mifflin Co., 1997), p. 160; *The Columbia Encyclopedia* (New York: Columbia University Press, 1993), p. 402.

4. *Information Please Almanac 1998*, ibid. See also George B.N. Ayittey, *Africa in Chaos* (New York: St. Martin's Press, 1998), p. 56; *Daily News*, Dar es Salaam, Tanzania, April – July 1972. I was a news reporter of the *Daily News* in Dar es Salaam when the massacres were taking place in Burundi during that period, forcing tens of thousands of refugees, mostly Hutu, to flee to Tanzania. We covered the crisis extensively and our newspaper became a valuable source of information about what was going on Burundi. I left for the United States in

November, the same year, to attend college.

5. Harvey Glickman, "Tanzania: From Disillusionment to Guarded Optimism," in *Current History: A Journal of Contemporary World Affairs*, May 1997, p. 218. See also Harvey Glickman, *Ethnic Conflict and Democratization in Africa* (Atlanta, Georgia: African Studies Association Press, 1995); Gérard Prunier, *The Rwanda Crisis: History of A Genocide* (New York: Columbia University Press, 1997); René Lemarchand, *Burundi: Ethnic Conflict and Genocide* (New York: Cambridge University Press, 1996); R. Lemarchand, *Burundi: Ethnocide as Discourse and Practice* (Cambridge: Cambridge University Press, 1994); Philip Gourevitch, *We Wish to Inform You That Tomorrow We Will Be Killed with Our Families: Stories from Rwanda* (New York: Farrar, Straus, and Giroux, 1998); Rosemond Halsey Carr with Ann Howard Halsey, *Land of A Thousand Hills: My Life in Rwanda* (New York: Viking, 1999).

6. Burundi, in *Reader's Digest: Almanac and Yearbook: 1986* (Pleasantville, New York: Reader's Digest Association, Inc., 1985), p. 517.

7. Michel Micombero, in *Africa Report*, September – October 1983, p. 35; *Daily News*, Dar es Salaam, Tanzania, 17 July 1983; *Daily Nation*, Nairobi, Kenya, 17 July 1983; *Le Monde*, Paris, 19 July 1983; *The New York Times*, 18 July 1983.

8. G.B.N. Ayittey, *Africa in Chaos*, op. cit., p. 56. See also G.B.N. Ayittey, *Africa Betrayed* (New York: St. Martin's Press, 1992).

9. *The Washington Post*, 17 April 1994, p. C – 2.

10. African leaders at a meeting in Arusha, Tanzania, in a statement quoted in "African Chiefs Seek Blockade of Burundi in Coup Protest," in the *International Herald Tribune*, 1 August 1996, p. 8.

11. Benjamin Mkapa, ibid.

12. "Burundi's Woe: Anybody There?" in *The Economist*, 27 July 1996, p. 37.

13. Ibid.

14. Ibid.

15. Burundi, in *The Wall Street Journal*, 5 August 1996, p. A-1, and 6 August 1996, p. A-1.

16. Tanzanian official, quoted in "Tanzanian Move to Block Oil Deliveries to Burundi," in the *International Herald Tribune*, 6 August 1996, p. 2.

17. Pierre Buyoya, ibid.

18. P. Buyoya, in *Le Figaro*, Paris, 7 August 1996; and in "UN Appeals to Africans to Allow Burundi Aid Shipments," in the *International Herald Tribune*, 8 August 1996, p. 2.

19. Ibid.

20. United Nations statement, ibid.

21. Paul Kagame, in an interview with BBC, quoted ibid.

22. "Burundi After the Coup," in *The Economist*, 3 August 1996, p. 35. See also Burundi, in "African Action," in *The Economist*, ibid., p. 4.

23. Ibid., p. 35.

24. Burundi, in *The Economist*, 17 August 1996, p. 4.

25. Ibid. See also Rwanda and Burundi, in *The Economist*, 10 August 1996, p. 4: "Rwanda's Tutsi-dominated government said it would not join other East African countries in imposing sanctions on the new Tutsi-led military regime in Burundi. The Burundian army was accused of massacres of Hutu civilians in a UN report."

26. "Organisation of African Unity (OAU) Conference: Resolution on Nigeria," in *Africa Research Bulletin*, Vol. V, London, September 1968, pp. 1171 et seq.; *Africa Contemporary Record: 1968 – 1969*, op. cit., p. 620.

27. Tanzanian officials, cited in *Sunday News*, Dar es Salaam, Tanzania, 11 August 1996; "UN Aid for Burundi Blocked at Port," in the *International Herald Tribune*, 12 August 1996, p. 7.

28. Luc Rukingama, quoted in "UN Aid for Burundi Blocked at Port," in the *International Herald Tribune*,

ibid.

29. Doctors Without Borders, cited ibid. See also "Nations Send an Important Message to Burundi – and to Africa," in the *International Herald Tribune*, 17 August 1996, p. 6.

30. "Stronger Sanctions Placed on Burundi," in the *International Herald Tribune*, ibid., p. 7.

31. Sylvestre Ntibantuganya, cited in "Ousted Leader Assails Regime in Burundi," in the *International Herald Tribune*, 20 August 1996, p. 10.

32. Ibid.

Part Three

1. "Hutu Flee Burundi Despite Assurances," in the *International Herald Tribune*, 21 August 1996, p. 2. See also *The Economist*, 24 August 1996, p. 4: "Thousands of Rwandan Hutu refugees fled from camps in Burundi claiming persecution by the army. Thousands of Zairean Tutsis, their citizenship denied, were driven out of eastern Zaire."

2. "Burundi Toll After Coup Put at 6,000," in the *International Herald Tribune*, 23 August 1996, p. 8.

3. Ibid.

4. "Bloodshed in Burundi: The Other War in Central Africa," in *The Economist,* 14 December 1996, p. 43.

5. "Don't Forget Burundi: Behind It Hovers the Spectre of Rwanda," in *The Economist*, 24 August 1996, p. 12.

6. Ibid.

7. Ibid.

8. Adrien Sibomana, quoted in "Fragile Burundi, 'Nation in Despair': U.S. and Aid Groups Cite Fears of a Surge in Mass Killings," in the *International Herald Tribune*, 26 August 1996, p. 9.

9. Thomas W. Lippman, on Burundi, in *The Washington Post*, 25 August 1996; and in "Fragile

Burundi, 'Nation in Despair,'" in the *International Herald Tribune*, ibid.

10. Pierre Buyoya, quoted in *Le Soir*, Brussels, Belgium, 27 August 1996; and in "Burundi's Leader Cautions Neighbors on Embargo," in the *International Herald Tribune*, 28 August 1996, p. 8.

11. Innocent Nimpagaritse, Hutu rebel spokesman, quoted in "Hutu Rebels Vow to Down Planes Flying into Burundi," in the *International Herald Tribune*, 29 August 1996, p. 2.

12. Jean-Luc Ndizeye, Burundi's military regime spokesman, ibid.

13. Jean-Baptiste Mbonyingingo, ibid.

14. "Battle Forces Foreigners to Flee Burundi Capital,"in the *International Herald Tribune*, 5 September 1996, p. 1.

15. Charles Mukasi, quoted in "Foes Play Down Burundi's End of Two Key Bans," in the *International Herald Tribune*, 14 September 1996, p. 2.

16. I. William Zartman, "Making Sense of East Africa's Wars," in *The Wall Street Journal*, 15 November 1996, p. A-14. See also "Africa's Approaching Catastrophe: Death Shadows Africa's Great Lakes....Why Are Hutus and Tutsis So Ready to Kill Each Other?" in *The Economist*, 19 October 1996, p. 45: "Genocide consumed Rwanda in 1994. Now, in another form, it threatens Burundi, maybe Zaire. Why are Hutus and Tutsis so ready to kill each other?....The relationship between Hutus and Tutsis goes deep into history....Hutus tell of centuries of enslavement by Tutsis. Tutsis say that...Hutus are playing racial politics." See also pp. 45 – 47, and 18, ibid.

17. "Africa's Approaching Catastrophe: Death Shadows Africa's Great Lakes," in *The Economist*, ibid.

18. Ibid.

19. Burundi, in *The Economist*, 7 December 1996, p. 4. See also Burundi, in *Current History: A Journal of Contemporary World Affairs*, December 1996, p. 443:

"October 28 – The Tutsi-dominated army admits that its soldiers killed at least 50 Hutu civilians in the southern province of Bururi on October 13; aid workers say more than 100 civilians were killed."

20. UN High Commissioner for Human Rights, Jose Ayala Lasso, in "UN Reports 1,100 Killings by Burundi Army and Asks Halt," in the *International Herald Tribune*, 12 December 1996, p. 8.

21. Ibid.

22. "Bloodshed in Burundi: The Other War in Central Africa," in *The Economist*, op. cit., p. 43.

23. Ibid.

24. Unnamed diplomat, ibid.

25. Ibid.

26. "Bloodshed in Burundi: The Other War in Central Africa," in *The Economist*, ibid., p. 44.

27. Julius Nyerere, "No Peace Without Justice, Which Is More Than Democracy," reprinted in the *International Herald Tribune*, 15 January 1997, p. 8. See also Nyerere in *The New York Times*, 14 and 15 January 1997.

28. Pierre Buyoya, in "Blood Rivalry Thwarts Burundi's Peace Quest," in the *International Herald Tribune*, 12 August 1997, p. 2. See also James C. McKinley, his report from Bujumbura, in *The New York Times*, 11 August 1997.

29. Ibid.

30. Charles Mukasi, ibid.

31. "Hutu Rebels Are Said to Clash in Burundi," in the *International Herald Tribune*, 13 August 1997, p. 1.

32. Mary Rose Habyamberi, in "Burundi Interns Hutu in Camps: Farmers Become the Victims of Crackdown on Guerrillas," in the *International Herald Tribune*, 14 August 1997, p. 2.

33. P. Buyoya, ibid.

34. "Burundi Interns Hutu in Camps," ibid.

35. Marcel Nyabenda, ibid.

36. Ancilla Ndayisenga, ibid.

37. UN official, ibid.

38. Quoted in "Africa's Approaching Catastrophe: Death Shadows Africa's Great Lakes," in *The Economist*, op. cit., p. 45.

39. Ibid.

40. "Fragile Four-Month Old Peace in Congo Appears Over," in *The Christian Science Monitor*, 8 November 1999, p. 24.

41. Julius Nyerere, quoted in "Talks Start Without Burundi," in the *International Herald Tribune*, 27 August 1997, p. 7.

42. *The Christian Science Monitor*, 28 October 1997, p. 2.

43..Jean-Bosco Daradangwe, in "Burundi Army Tracks Hutu Attackers," in the *International Herald Tribune*, 2 January 1998, p. 7.

44. *The Economist*, 10 January 1998, p. 4.

45. Mamert Sinaranzi, cited in "Hutu Raid Army Base in Burundi: At Least 150 Civilians Reported Killed in Battle," in *The Boston Globe*, 2 January 1998, p. A-2.

46. Jean-Luc Ndizye, ibid.

47. "Hutu Raid Army Base in Burundi," in *The Boston Globe,* ibid.

48. J.B. Daradangwe, cited in "Burundi Army Tracks Hutu Attackers," in the *International Herald Tribune*, op. cit., p. 7.

49. M. Sinaranzi, ibid.

50. Christophe Nkurunziza, "Survivors Aid Burundi Search for Attackers," in *The Boston Globe*, 4 January 1998, p. A-18.

51. "Africa's Approaching Catastrophe," in *The Economist*, op. cit., p. 47. See also the Tutsi in *Africa Analysis: The Fortnightly Bulletin on Financial and Political Trends*, No. 259, London, 1 November 1996, p. 15.

52. "Burundi's Cruel Civil War: Pawns in the War," in *The Economist*, 10 January 1998, pp. 37, and 38.

53. "Hutu Rebels Kill 45 in Two Burundi Attacks," in the *International Herald Tribune*, 22 January 1998, p. 6.

54. "Burundi Official Killed in Crash," in the International Herald Tribune, 29 January 1998, p. 11.

55. Pierre-Claver Ndayicariye, cited in "Copter Crash Kills Burundi Defense Chief, Four Others," in The Boston Globe, 29 January 1998, p. A-6.

56. Burundi, in *Keesing's Record of World Events*, January 1998, p. 41991. See also pp. 41950, and 41897.

57. Athanase Nibizi, in "Burundi Rebels Said to Kill 24 in Attack on Village," in *The Boston Globe,* 12 February 1998, p. A-23.

58. Zacharie Kamwenubusa, ibid.

59. Ibid.

60. Reuters, ibid.

61. Burundi, in *Current History: A Journal of Contemporary World Events*, April 1998, p. 189.

62. "73 in Burundi Reported Dead in Hutu Rebel Raid," in *The Boston Globe*, 23 April 1998, p. A-24.

63. Ibid.

64. Daniel arap Moi, cited in "Moi Urges Separation of Tutsi and Hutu," in the *International Herald Tribune*, 10 April 1998, p. 6.

65. "63 Reported Killed in Burundi Camps," in the *International Herald Tribune*, 20 May 1997, p. 6.

66. Burundi, in *The Christian Science Monitor*, 8 May 1998, p. 2.

67. Leonidas Ntibayazi, in "Signing of Constitution Sets Stage for Burundi's Reforms," in *The Boston Globe*, 7 June 1998, p. A-27.

68. Ambroise Niyonsaba, ibid.

69. "Burundi Military and Rebels Disagree Over a Cease-fire," in The Boston Globe, 18 June 1998, p. A-28.

70. "Burundi on the Brink of Peace?," in *The Economist*, 20 June 1998, p. 49.

71. "Refugees Flee Burundi Crashes," in The Boston Globe, 1 August 1998, p. A-7. See also Burundi, in

Current History: A Journal of Contemporary World Affairs, September 1998, p. 289.

72. Burundi, in The Christian Science Monitor, 13 November 1998, p. 2.

73. "Burundi: new Spate of Killings," in *Keesing's Record of World Events*, November 1998, 42599. See also p. 42540.

74. East Africans Drop Burundi Sanctions," in the *International Herald Tribune*, 25 January 1999, p. 4; *The New York Times*, 24 January 1999; *The Economist*, 30 January 1999, p.4.

75. *The Economist*, 20 March 1999, p. 6.

76. "Five Sentenced to Death in Burundi Murder," in the *International Herald Tribune*, 15 May, 1999, p. 2.

77. Ibid.

78. "Burundi: Convictions in President's Death," in *The New York Times*, 15 May 1999, p. A-4; *The Economist*, 22 May 1999, p. 6.

79. *The Economist,* 14 August 1999, p. 4.

80. "Burundi's Army Killed Hutu, Villagers Say," in the *International Herald Tribune*, 13 August 1999, p. 1.

81. *The Christian Science Monitor*, 30 August 1999, p. 20.

82. *The Economist*, 4 September 1999, p. 10. See also, "In Burundi, 9 Die in Attack on UN Convoy," in the *International Herald Tribune*, 13 October 1996, p. 6:

"Nine people were killed Tuesday (12 October 1999) when Hutu rebels attacked a UN relief convoy in southern Burundi, a spokesman for the Burundi Army said....An extremist Hutu organization known as PALIPEHUTU has recently warned all expatriates in Burundi to leave the country or face attack.

It was not clear which rebel group carried out the attack, but Colonel Longin Minani said he was certain that the attackers had come from their base in neighboring Tanzania.

Several Hutu rebel organizations that operate out of

both Congo and Tanzania are trying to oust the Tutsi-dominated government of President Pierre Buyoya. Since the Hutu rebels recently stepped up their attacks in areas outside the capital (Bujumbura), the government has forcibly moved at least 250,000 Hutu civilians from their homes and into what it calls 'protected sites.'

Colonel Minani has said the Hutu civilians are being transferred to the camps to protect them from rebel pressure to support their cause as well as to clear the way for the army to flush out the rebels.

Both the European Union (EU) and the United States have criticized the forced relocation of civilians, and the World Food Program said last week that it was distributing food to the camps on a 'critical need basis.'"

See also "UN Workers in Burundi Were Slain on a Whim," in the *International Herald Tribune*, 14 October 1999, pp. 1, and 8: "The Burundi government, which is dominated by an elite sliver of the minority Tutsi population, has responded (to rebel attacks) by moving large numbers of Hutus off their land while the army sweeps the countryside. More than a quarter of a million people have been confined to 'regrouping' camps. Conditions are said to be wretched, and international agencies have pressed for relief."

See also Burundi, in *Current History: A Journal of Contemporary World Affairs*, October 1999, p. 348.

83. Nyerere, in *The Economist*, 16 October 1999, p. 4; "Obituary: Julius Nyerere, Africa's Failed Idealist," in *The Economist*, 23 October 1999, p. 101.

84. "Nyerere: A Good Heart," in *Newsweek*, 25 October 1999, p. 8.

85. "Julius Nyerere Dies in London," in *The Christian Science Monitor,* 15 October 1999, p. 24. See also Nyerere, in the *International Herald Tribune*, *The Washington Post*, 15 October 1999.

86. Keith B. Richburg, *Out of America: A Black Man Confronts Africa* (New York: Basic Books, Harper Collins,

1997), p. 241.

87. Julius Nyerere, "Why We Recognised Biafra," in *The Observer*, London, 28 April 1968; reprinted in Colin Legum and John Drysdale, eds., *Africa Contemporary Record: Annual Survey and Documents 1968 – 1969* (London: Africa Research Ltd., 1969), pp. 651 – 652.

88. "Room for Optimism in a Churning Africa," in *The Christian Science Monitor*, 18 October 1999, p. 10.

89. Julius Nyerere of Tanzania Dies; Preached African Socialism to the World," in *The New York Times*, 15 October 1999, p. B-10.

90. "Burundi's Even Uneasier Peace: Murder and Manhunts," in *The Economist*, 23 October 1999, p. 50:

"The fighting nowadays is low-intensity but it remains vicious, marked by massacres and arbitrary killings....

(When) President Pierre Buyoya seized power, for the second time, in 1996,...he presented himself as a model military reformer, committed to building an alliance of moderate Tutsis and Hutus, isolating the extremists on both sides.

Peace talks were started in Arusha, Tanzania, under the chairmanship of Julius Nyerere. Sanctions were lifted in January (1999), and hopes rose for a settlement by the end of the year, after Mr. Buyoya's promise of a 'government of partnership' and a transition to civilian democracy.

But the death last week of Mr. Nyerere casts doubt on the prospects for peace, which had already been badly undermined by violence. The government blames the two main rebel groups, the Forces for the Defence of Democracy (FDD), and the Party for the Liberation of the Hutu People (PALIPEHUTU). Moderate wings of both movements have been brought into the Arusha negotiations, but the militants remain outside them."

Without the inclusion and participation of the militants in the peace process, there will be no peace in Burundi. The leaders of my country, Tanzania, should know that. The same applies to Rwanda. In Burundi alone, several thousand people were killed in 1999. And more people are going to be killed.

False accusations also help fuel the conflict. For example, not long after nine people were killed on 12 October 1999 in an attack on a UN relief convoy in the southern part of Burundi, relief workers disputed the government's claim that it was certain the attackers were Hutu rebels who had come from their base in neighbouring Tanzania. Instead, the international relief workers and their Burundian counterparts blamed the Tutsi-dominated government for the cold-blooded murders of the UN relief workers.

See "Crackdown on Burundi Rebels Forces 350,000 Hutu into Camps," in the *International Herald Tribune*, 28 December 1999, pp. 1 and 4:

"On October 12, two UN workers, one with the World Food Program and the other with UNICEF, were executed in southeastern Burundi. The government identified several rebels as the killers, although many aid officials suspect the (Tutsi) army itself"; cf., "In Burundi, 9 Die in Attack on UN Convoy," in the *International Herald Tribune*, 13 October 1999, p. 6.

Made in the USA
Lexington, KY
23 April 2014